# GARDENING
## IN A
## SMALL
## SPACE

Lance Hattatt

Illustrations by
Elaine Franks

This is a Parragon Publishing Book
This edition published in 2000

Parragon Publishing
Queen Street House
4 Queen Street
Bath BA1 1HE, UK

Conceived, edited, illustrated
and produced by Robert Ditchfield Publishers

The illustrations on pages 56 and 57 are by Brenda Stephenson.

ISBN 0 7525 3469 6 (Hardback)
ISBN 0 7525 3582 X (Paperback)

A copy of the British Library Cataloguing in Publication
Data is available from the Library.

Typeset by Action Publishing Technology Ltd, Gloucester
Colour origination by Colour Quest Graphic Services Ltd,
London E9
Printed and bound in Indonesia

*Half Title*: The award winning small garden featured on page 68.

*Frontispiece*: Mirabel Osler's town garden, described on page 62.

*Opposite*: The water feature in 'A Garden of Pots' on page 116.

# GARDENING
## IN A
# SMALL SPACE

# THIS BOOK

aims to show the reader how even a small space can be made into a garden of refuge and charm.

It begins by looking at features and styles that are appropriate to limited areas. The central section then considers in detail eleven gardens. Some of these are very small, but even the larger ones are subdivided into spaces that have been designed on a small scale. These gardens help put the features and styles of the first section into context as well as providing inspiring ideas for those wishing to start a new garden.

The final section deals with planting a small space. Naturally many plants of small size are included but there are also larger subjects which can be kept within bounds by pruning and cutting back and which will become valuable members of the small garden.

## SYMBOLS

Where measurements are given, the first is the plant's height followed by its spread.
The following symbols are also used in this book:

- ○ = thrives best or only in full sun
- ◑ = thrives best or only in part-shade
- ● = succeeds in full shade
- E = evergreen

Where no sun symbol and no reference to sun or shade is made in the text, it can be assumed that the plant tolerates sun or light shade.

## POISONOUS PLANTS

Many plants are poisonous and it must be assumed that no part of a plant should be eaten unless it is known that it is edible.

# Contents

Right: A view of the gravel garden featured on page 92.

# Gardening in a Small Space

Increasingly more and more people find themselves gardening in a small space. As land values have soared and house prices spiralled, so the opportunity of owning a large garden becomes less and less. This, together with a move away from the openness of the countryside to the comparative restriction of town and city, has meant a complete reappraisal of gardening technique and style. Coupled to this is a marked change in the use of leisure time where, today, so many extra demands are placed upon the individual that, however willing, there is simply insufficient time and resources available to manage the more spacious gardens of yesterday.

But this is not to decry the future, to suggest that things were, somehow or other, better in the past. Far from it. Gardening today is at its most exciting ever. New plant introductions, the accessibility of specialist nurseries and garden centres, splendid books of reference, favourite magazines, wonderful gardens open to the public, all of these, and much more, serve to encourage, enthuse and inspire the gardener no matter what the size of plot.

## FACING UP TO CHALLENGES

A limited space does, of course, bring with it its own particular challenges, requiring imaginative and flexible management and organizational skills. Gardens which may be seen in their entirety throughout the year in all seasons demand original and innovative ideas if interest is to be maintained at all times. Aesthetics play a major part too, for it is important that the materials and artefacts used in the garden are not simply appropriate, but well suited to their surroundings.

Small gardens inevitably restrict choice. A tiny space, sadly, does not allow for the cultivation of every garden-worthy plant. Nor does it admit all design features anymore than it accommodates every style. Instead, it calls for self-discipline, for the formulation of clear, often simple, solutions and for the ability to work and rework ideas until they present a cohesive, unified whole. But in this lies much of the fun and enjoyment. The application of firm, confident judgement will reward with a garden, however short on space, that is not only pleasing to the eye but, most importantly, which reflects the energy and personal vision of its owner.

Privacy is, understandably, always a consideration. And where the garden becomes a very real, and much used, extension to the indoors, then account should be taken of this at the planning stage. Similarly a balance must be drawn between the garden purely as a place of beauty and somewhere that has an effective, functional purpose. Discrete areas will need to be found for compost, for household rubbish, for the storing of tools and garden machinery, for fuel, as well as for garden furniture, cold frames, old pots and such similar items.

All available space has been artfully utilized here in front of this stone cottage to provide a succession of colour lasting right through the summer and into the autumn. Note how annuals are mixed with perennials to extend the season of interest.

Against the walls themselves colourful window boxes and hanging baskets are set off by the green foliage of the climbing creeper. Later this will turn a fiery red.

A small lawn, raised borders, closely packed with an arrangement of interesting plants, and an ancient fruit tree provide the perfect setting for outdoor meals in this tiny city garden. Dappled shade is particularly welcome during the hot days of summer.

The small garden must, as a matter of course, be all-purpose. It cannot, nor should it, cater for the needs of the gardener alone but should aim to provide for other family members as well. Where there are young children, then a play area with room for a sandpit, swings or climbing frame may be a necessity. For others, a space in which to relax, to entertain friends, to enjoy meals outside, perhaps a barbeque. For an older person, possibly a small greenhouse in which to potter, somewhere to take cuttings or raise seedlings. There may indeed be divided loyalties. One person wishes only to grow flowers, to have an ornamental garden, another vegetables, a productive one.

Compromises will have to be reached, but it is through these that the garden will adopt its own identity and, ultimately, be in harmony with its owner.

### ASSESSING THE SITE

Aspect, the way in which a garden faces, will be of greater significance in a small area. A large garden will, on account of its very size, have both sunny and shady spots. Ideally this will be the case in the small garden, but it may not necessarily be so. Surrounding buildings, a neighbouring tree or trees, or simply the wrong aspect may well result in an overall lack of sunshine. On the other hand, it may be that the site is very open and exposed to the sun and will, accordingly, be hot and dry. Both of these situations will largely dictate the kinds of plants that may be grown if plantings are to thrive and the garden succeed.

Soil type will be another determining factor in deciding which plants to grow. The degree of alkalinity or acidity of the soil, measured on a pH scale, is an indicator of what will flourish. A pH of 7.0 equals a neutral soil, above is alkaline, below acid. Some plants such as rhododendrons, pieris and summer-flowering heathers, will not tolerate lime and will only succeed on acid soils with a low pH. Others, like bearded irises and paeonies, seem to prefer some lime content. Whatever, the vast majority of plants are unfussy and will, if well tended, grow quite happily. Most garden centres sell simple but effective soil testing kits so that it is relatively easy to ascertain soil type with a high degree of accuracy.

Small gardens, which are usually but not always enclosed, create their own micro-climate. It is often the case that the temperature, in both summer and winter, may be noticeably different within the garden from that outside. Sheltering buildings, walls, fences, even foliage, all combine to bring about a small-scale 'greenhouse' effect. The result is that it may be possible to cultivate successfully more of those plants which are generally thought to be on the borderline of hardiness. However, one has to admit that some gardens may well, on account of their situation, be particularly exposed to cold and suffer as frost pockets. Wind chill, as damaging as the sharpest of frosts, is something else to

A narrow path between buildings, as here, can often form a wind tunnel. Strong winds trapped can cause considerable damage to plants which stand in their way.

be considered. Very often the gap between buildings, usually quite narrow, forms a wind tunnel exposing anything within its path to winter gusts and gales. Where this is the case it may be necessary to devise some kind of shield or screening to lessen the impact of the wind.

## CREATING STYLE

Taking over an existing garden is sometimes less easy than beginning from nothing. Inevitably there will be permanent structures and features which will have to be incorporated into any new plan. Some it may be possible, and desirable, to highlight, others will need to be concealed. Do not be afraid to dispense with anything unwanted, the removal of which is practical. It is much easier to be ruthless early on than to live with something which, ultimately, is going to distract from the overall effect. Creating an individual style of the garden which is allowed to become a dominant and recurring theme will result in something which not only makes a statement but in so doing presents a picture of unity. What style is chosen will, of course, be a matter of personal choice and taste. It may be that an old-fashioned, cottage garden look, currently popular, will particularly appeal where the emphasis is on an informal mixture of fruit, flowers and vegetables. On the other hand, you may prefer a garden which is severely formal, relying particularly on structure, in the form of clipped hedges and walls, and an eye to symmetry where flowers as such play a secondary rôle. Alternatively, a garden arranged for seasonal colour, or one of muted foliage effects, may be what is in mind. In essence, none of this matters. What is important is that the finished garden suggests a distinctive style which is consistent and readily identifiable.

Scale, the ratio by which one object is related to another, is certainly one of the most difficult things to balance correctly when planning the outside. And yet it is an area which it is unwise to ignore completely. Try to look at everything — garden buildings, hard landscaping, trees,

This garden, awarded a gold medal at the Chelsea Flower Show, amply demonstrates how much of interest may be fitted into a very small area. Plant material, appropriate to the space, is arranged with the eye of an artist.

A narrow border tightly filled with, in the main, colourful annuals. The effect of this kind of planting is heightened, as in this case, when the colour image is restricted.

## CREATIVE PLANTING

Where planting is concerned, small gardens concentrate the mind. Limited space of necessity forces selection with every plant having to earn, and in some cases doubly earn, its place within the whole scheme. Focus on those which are reliable, which perform well and which, if possible, contribute interest over an extended period. Trees, for example, may be chosen not just for leaf but also for flower, interesting bark and possible autumn colour. Shrubs to include are those which, in addition to unusual flowers, produce berries at the year's end or which may be evergreen. Both, of course, make excellent hosts for all manner of climbers, not least clematis. Even perennial flowers may have particularly fine foliage to be followed with unusual and dramatic seed-heads.

shrubs, perennial plantings – not in isolation but in the ways in which they are in proportion one with another. This is particularly so in establishing a connection, however slight it may appear, between house and garden and is equally important when it comes to the placing of all plant material as well as garden ornament.

Colour, one of the most pleasing aspects of any garden, needs to be handled in a small space with the utmost care if a spotty, unco-ordinated look is to be avoided. It may well prove wise to restrict colours singly or to similar or contrasting tints and tones of the colour wheel. Such application calls for a considerable amount of self-discipline but can produce most worthwhile results. Indeed, form and the texture of foliage, not to mention scent, are as demanding of attention as is the arrangement of flower colour.

Take advantage of any vertical surfaces to double as supports for climbing plants. These may include the more obvious house and garage walls, the uprights of sheds and greenhouses, summerhouses, fences, garden walls, pergolas and arbours as well as less immediately apparent trunks of trees, sides of hedges and all fastigiate plants. Horizontals too, such as the uppermost areas of shrubs, fixed ropes and wires, the very tops of boundary walls and fences, may all be employed as homes to climbers.

Planting need not be confined to traditional borders. Raised beds, forming attractive features in their own right, may be used to accommodate a whole range of plants for which there may otherwise be insufficient space. They are especially good for alpines and those subjects which are in need of sharp drainage. All manner of containers, from terracotta pots and classical urns to troughs and discarded sinks, can be employed either singly or in groups to form attractive, colourful arrangements. An advantage of this kind of gardening is that pots may be set aside, or replanted, once their season of interest has passed. Do not overlook the potential of exterior walls. As well as being clothed in climbers, they may be furnished with hanging pots, baskets or window boxes to lift and brighten what might be dismissed as uninteresting façades.

For those with a spirit of adventure, it is possible to shape any number of evergreens into imaginative works. Yew and box are most commonly used for topiary but holly, shrubby honeysuckles, Portuguese laurel, bay and ivy may all be trimmed and trained successfully and effectively.

Gardening in a small space may, for you, be nothing greater than a few pots displayed on a balcony or window sill. That matters not at all. In fact the smallest gardens ever are those usually to be found in a horticultural tent at a village fête in summer. Consisting of a seed tray filled with soil they conspire to include a handful of gravel for paths, mossy lawns, twiggy fences and tiny, tiny borders planted out with miniature dianthus and aromatic thymes. A child's offering each may be, they nonetheless embody the essential ingredients for any garden anywhere and from observing them, as in closely looking at all gardens everywhere, we may all learn to strive towards that ultimate happiness and contentment which is the reward of all gardening.

Tiny gardens need not, nor should they be, without interest. This one makes excellent use of foliage plants, which, overspilling the path, convey a sense of plenty yet are, at the same time, relaxing to the eye.

# Patios and Paved Areas

For many people gardening in a really small area a traditional lawn would not only be inappropriate and out of place but also totally impractical. Paving, in one form or another, is an ideal solution allowing access to the garden in all weathers and at all times of year.

In some instances space may be so limited as to restrict all plants to pot cultivation. In other situations it may be possible to surround a patio or terrace area with beds or borders or even to allow for planting spaces in the hard surface itself.

Old flagstones, granite sets, cobbles, brick and gravel all make for attractive and interesting hard-landscaping and may be combined to form surfaces which are varied and detailed in an unusual manner. Where reclaimed brick and stone may prove to be too expensive, a wide range of cheaper but very acceptable reproduction materials is readily available. An alternative is to use treated wooden planks as decking. These make for a durable, hard wearing surface which looks especially good in a contemporary setting.

Reproduction paving stones have been used informally in this patio garden to form a winding path through the borders and to surface an area designed for outdoor meals. Timber pillars are used as supports for climbing plants.

Sun streams into this corner where trellis over fencing and a painted arbour unite to trap the heat. Planting is arranged to mask the edges of the paving, the cracks of which are home to tiny self-seeders.

Carefully controlled colour is the inspiration behind this randomly paved terraced area which immediately adjoins the house. Frothy lady's mantle, *Alchemilla mollis*, is allowed to seed at will, as are poppies and violas. Large pots, heavily planted, complete the picture.

A nice touch has been to surround the terrace with a band of cobbles (see bottom right of picture). Mixing materials in a restrained way adds considerable interest.

A very modern design like this one depends entirely for its success on the bold execution of a relatively simple idea. Here a series of permanent containers are planted alike, relying on repetition for effect. Flower colour is chosen to harmonize with the paving.

Gravel, into which plants are allowed to grow, contrasts with regularly shaped paving to give this modern garden a clear sense of purpose. The straight line of the path leading to the pair of box-filled planters introduces a note of formality.

Surround a seat, such as this one, with pots full of summer flowering lilies. These are excellent for cultivation in containers where they should be kept well watered during the growing season. Dead head blooms as they fade and cut down stems in autumn when a liquid feed will help to build up the strength of bulbs for the following year.

# Seats in Small Gardens

Of course gardening is about work but it should, equally, be concerned with relaxation. This is especially so of the small garden which so often doubles as an outside room either for sitting or eating outdoors.

Seats in small gardens need to be multi-purpose. On the one hand they must be aesthetically pleasing, to look attractive and inviting and to fit in with their surroundings. On the other hand, they are required to be functional, to fit their purpose, to be robust, weather resistant and long lasting.

Natural or painted wood, metal, stone and plastic are all materials which come to little harm if exposed to the elements. Basket, cane, canvas or material covered cushions must all be given some form of protection against wet and will need to be housed indoors over winter.

Painted furniture, other than ubiquitous white, can give expression to the wildest fantasy and colour can be simply and speedily changed to fit a different mood or season.

Although this seat is a perfect resting place, its principal purpose is as a focal point within a small garden. The Chinese Chippendale design to the back follows a traditional pattern. White tulips in spring complement the overall effect.

A well crafted rustic seat which is accommodated into a small alcove set between stone walls. Overhanging shrubs, which are allowed in part to obscure the timbers, enhance an atmosphere of timelessness. The owners of this garden have succeeded in conveying to this area the appearance and feeling of a corner of a much grander garden.

# Containers

Pots and containers, of virtually every description, are an absolute necessity for those who garden in very limited spaces. It is tempting to say that there is not anything which cannot be grown in a pot and whilst this is obviously not strictly true, it is often very surprising what will succeed given the right conditions.

Good drainage is essential if you are to be successful with plants in pots. In containers designed for some other purpose several open drainage holes must be made in the bottom. Over these a layer of crocks, put in before the compost and any planting takes place, will prevent the growing medium from becoming water-logged.

Plants need to fit their pots. Plants will not cultivate root growth in containers which are too large nor will they thrive in situations where their roots become pot bound. A programme of regular feeding, and watering during the summer months, is necessary to grow healthy, disease-free plants.

A clever arrangement of window boxes, placed at various heights, and an assortment of pots are home to this colourful display which partially masks the front wall of this stone cottage.

Note how plant material has been artfully selected and arranged to conceal all sight of the containers.

Several inches of concrete was no obstacle (see 'A Garden of Pots' page 116) when it came to clothing walls with ivy. An old chimney is put into service.

Hostas are excellent subjects for pots and to grow them in this way is to avoid slug damage to the leaves.

Spring bedding, consisting of bright-eyed pansies and yellow tulips, looks particularly well in this handsome, classical urn. Colour in the urn is deliberately chosen to pick up the tones of the bracts of the euphorbia massed behind.

Yet again the ingenuity of the owners of 'A Garden of Pots' (see page 116) is put to the test. The projecting roof of the outhouses forms a shelf upon which are placed a number of colourful pots. Foliage plants are deliberately mixed with those bright with flower.

Plants grown in fairly inaccessible positions, like these ones, really do need some form of automatic watering system.

*Solanum rantonnetii*, a tender climber, is positioned during the summer months at the base of a flight of steps in 'A Gravel Garden' (see page 92). Throughout the winter it is placed in the frost free conservatory.

A pot grown agave forms the centrepiece of this walled courtyard garden which, although enclosed, attracts the sun. *Verbena* 'Homestead Purple', grown annually from cuttings, gives a touch of colour. The agave requires protection in winter.

Bay trees lend themselves to being treated as standards. This one, with fine twisted stem, is grown in a darkly painted Versailles tub surrounded by pale lilac flowered pansies in season.

*Santolina*, or cotton lavender, flourishes in this large, glazed stoneware pot which is positioned as an eye-catcher at the end of a short, cobbled path. In fact this pot would look equally good empty.

A beautifully proportioned, pleasingly decorated jar which is of sufficient size as to be included in this pretty garden scene on its own merits. In winter it will be starkly etched against the stone wall.

Mirabel Osler (see page 62) has included this stone pot in her town garden purely as a piece of decoration. Surrounded with both foliage and flowering plants it forms part of an attractive composition.

Home-grown strawberries are the very being of summer and may be
cultivated most successfully in a clay strawberry planter. Even before
the ripening of the fruits the foliage, and then the flower, is
appealing. A handsome pot like this one could be placed beside the
back door, on the patio or terrace, or as the focal point of a tiny
vegetable or herb garden.

Nothing could be simpler than this shallow dish filled with various forms of houseleek. Easy to grow, they thrive on neglect and appear not to suffer if left unwatered during dry periods.

A stone trough has been utilized here to form a miniature scree bed for tiny succulents. Small fragments of stone have been set among the plants to emphasize form and scale. The top surface is dressed with horticultural grit to give a neat appearance.

An entire rock garden, beautifully planted, and all arranged in an antique stone trough. A cerise coloured phlox cannot escape notice, in marked contrast to the more sober miniature irises which are about to flower in the background.

Small-growing varieties of hardy geranium need not be thought unsuitable for growing in a container. In this instance they look particularly good planted on their own. A top dressing of grit serves to improve drainage.

A bar running across the window sill provides a built-in support for a collection of pots. Decorating the outside of windows, often with purpose-made boxes, is a simple but effective solution to gardening without a garden. Always, of course, ensure that fixings are secure.

Plants packed tightly together guarantee that any display looks purposeful. Flowers included in the window box are repeated at ground level.

The façade of this town house is greatly enlivened with this collection of summer bedding all contained within a single window box.

Cool whites, creams and blues are included together in this very sophisticated, imaginative and well planted window box. To keep plants in this condition means regular feeding and watering.

Another very thoughtful and carefully considered scheme. Here hot reds and purples, some blatantly clashing, are kept in check with fresh green foliage. Trailing ivy has, very cleverly, been encouraged to spill down the wall in a series of swags.

Window boxes do not have to be for summer only. This one, consisting of foliage plants, will appear just as attractive in mid-winter.

Hanging baskets are huge fun and give scope to all manner of plant combinations. Bought ready prepared, or filled yourself, they will add sparkle to even the dullest of spots. Remember, they require copious amounts of water.

These baskets are arranged over a terrace which is in frequent use as an outdoor dining room during hot summer months.

This hanging basket has been prepared with spring in mind. After the bleak days of winter, what could be more welcoming?

A plain brick wall becomes the focus of attention with this brightly coloured hanging basket beside an entrance door.

*Fuchsia* 'Miss California' is of the softest of pinks. The plain wall of this conservatory heightens its charming simplicity.

# Paths

In the majority of gardens paths represent one of the major aspects of hard landscaping. As a general rule they fall into two categories. First, those which are primarily functional and which are a direct means of getting from one part of the garden to another. Secondly, those which are included for their decorative value, usually designed to provide a visual link between separate areas.

Materials from which paths may be formed are many and varied. The final choice will depend largely on the purpose of the path, its situation and frequency of use. Old flagstones or bricks, laid in a variety of patterns, always look good but are, sadly, expensive. Both are inclined to be slippery in wet weather. Gravel is a very much cheaper substitute but needs to be contained within an edging. Cobbles and granite sets look very effective and are now readily available as modern reproductions. Cinder or bark paths are ideally suited to any informal situation.

Within a small space, such as this little enclosed garden, the path takes on an important rôle. Serving two functions, it is intended both for decoration as well as for access and is therefore constructed of materials which are pleasing to look at as well as being hard wearing. The way in which the brick edging has been incorporated into the cobbles as diamonds greatly adds to the interest and appeal.

Paths do not, of course, have to be continuous. Here a series of flagstones is set at intervals through a border, the gaps in between having been generously carpeted with the blue-leafed form of acaena.

A sympathetic treatment of a path for a herb garden which makes imaginative use of reclaimed materials. Some thought has been given to the width which is wide enough to allow the free passage of a wheelbarrow.

The whole of this garden has been shaped by the positioning of paths and steps. Materials are the same for both in order to give a feeling of unity in what is, after all, a small area. Plants are allowed to spill out over the edges, thus avoiding any hard lines. Pastel colours are chosen for the way in which they too soften the scheme.

# Changes of Level

Steps in any garden, however small, and whether by design or through necessity, invite an immediate response. Here is a different area to be explored, there a change of mood. Climb up and there is a sense of achievement, of reaching a goal. Descend and the way is unknown, fully of mystery and excitement.

Construction may be of the simplest. A few timbers set as risers into a sloping site, the treads of compacted earth, will, in the right situation, be as appropriate as is a flight of stone steps complete with balustrade elsewhere. Try to match the treatment of any change of level to the atmosphere and feeling, and indeed situation, of your garden. Straight flights of cut stone are best reserved for where you intend formality. Narrow, twisting steps fit better into an informal, more relaxed garden.

Always satisfy yourself that any steps are safe, are well marked and are lit if they are to be used at night. Where a change of level is steep it may be advisable to include a handrail.

Good quality engineering bricks have been used as the basis for this short flight of steps leading from the garden to the terrace. Shallow risers, over which ivy is trained, allow effortless movement from one level to another.

This broad flight of steps is one of the main points of interest of 'A Gravel Garden' (see page 92). Tiny plants, surviving on very little depth of soil, have been encouraged to fill the cracks. Planted pots add further interest.

These steps, wide at the top approach, draw the visitor down from the upper level at the house into the garden proper. A seat in the far distance acts as a magnet.

Simply constructed, yet completely practical, these steps make use of rough sawn timbers, which have been pegged, as rivets, and gravel for treads. Naturalized bluebells growing at the sides contribute to the woodland air.

Elegant stairs, complete with iron railings, mark the entrance to this town house. To divide the property from another, the boundary has been planted out with a series of boxes designed to follow the line and level of the steps. Evergreen ivies and small shrubs guarantee that interest is not just seasonal.

# *Water Features*

Water in a garden is particularly appealing. Whether as a small, trickling stream, or as a formal pool or as a natural pond, it is bound to excite interest. Placing a water feature within a large garden presents few problems. In a small space the choice becomes much more limited and care has to be exercised to see that everything remains in scale.

Today with the availability of all manner of electric pumps for fountains and spouts, with preformed streams and ponds, with liners available in all sizes, it is possible to find something which is suited to the tiniest of gardens. Even a small pot water feature, surrounded by pebbles and with a small pump recycling water from a hidden bowl, will enliven the garden with its splash or spray.

Before coming to any decision, visit a garden centre or, better still, a water garden specialist. There you will be able to see at first hand the wide range of water features available and should be able to take advantage of knowledgeable and informed advice. A word of caution. Any water installation requiring electricity should be carried out by a qualified electrician.

Planting around a pond or along the length of a stream can be enormous fun. Remember, the ground will not necessarily be moisture retentive so choose plants which, whilst looking particularly good in association with water, are unfussy about type of soil and situation.

The edges of this small pond are completely masked with generous plantings of marginal perennials. Bright yellow flowers of *Trollius chinensis* 'Golden Queen' add a touch of late spring cheer.

Even the tiniest of gardens need not be without water in some form. This ivy edged pool and fountain belong in 'A Green Town Garden' (see page 88). Water irises give colour in due season.

A tranquil oasis has been created in this city garden where a formal pool becomes a dominant feature. An emphasis on green contributes to the cool, calm atmosphere, successfully blocking out the hurly-burly of life outside.

Pots strategically placed around the pool are used to introduce a note of colour. Such flexibility allows for periodic changes of interest.

Very much a rock pool, the construction of this feature makes extensive use of natural stone which has been carefully laid to suggest a natural outcrop. The fresh, ferny leaves of the acer, which in time will overhang the water, are entirely in keeping.

This kidney-shaped garden pool incorporates a tiny stream and waterfall, the running water helping to keep the surface clear. Large, flat stones form an edge and merge successfully into the rockery on the far side. A ribbon of gravel acts as a mowing strip.

Ponds like this one are best sited in a sunny spot which is not overshadowed by trees. This eliminates autumn debris falling into the water.

Springtime and the rock garden comes into its own. This is the season of the year when so many alpines and rockery plants give of their best. The arrangement of this rock garden is particularly effective for it allows for the inclusion of a tiny stream as well as a small fountain. Both of these, operated by a concealed electrical pump, will continue to provide interest long after the alpine flowers have faded. Something along these lines would not be difficult to copy and could readily be fitted into the smallest of spaces.

Designed as a round, this pond fits happily into the top terrace of 'Terracing a Hillside' (see page 96). A golden leafed bamboo acts as an eye-catcher against the house wall, the colour picked up in the leaves of the hosta.

'A Garden Designer's Garden' (see page 78) is home to this circular pond which, in turn, is home to a family of goldfish. Close to a sitting out area, it forms a pleasant feature.

Possibly the simplest of all water features and one which is most suitable for any situation. These water lilies float contentedly on the surface of an old metal basin removed from a scrapyard.

An arrangement of mask, and container to catch the water, like this one, is simple to install yet brings to the garden that wonderful, musical sound of running water.

This inspired and fascinating water feature, nicely positioned within a pattern of granite sets, provides a cooling effect on a hot summer's day. A submersible pump, placed in a tank below the millstone, allows for the water to be recycled.

A pot fountain surrounded by carefully placed stones and larger rocks is a delightful addition to the corner of this small town garden. An eye for detail has been exercised in keeping everything in proportion.

An imaginative touch has been to place the terracotta jar on its side where it spills out a trickle of pea gravel.

# Colourful Bedding

For sheer brilliance of flower colour, nothing can compare with the exuberance of massed bedding where the brightest of oranges, yellows and reds vie with each other for attention and position. This is not gardening for the faint hearted but for those who want to enliven a dull space, to bring cheer to the darkest of days and who wish always to be reminded of long, hot sunny hours.

Bedding out need not be confined only to summer. Winter flowering pansies, whose cheerful faces will defy even the worst of weather, will bloom continuously over the coldest period to be replaced in spring with a wonderful mixture of annuals and bulbs. Indeed, if you select with care, then it should be possible to have colour in the garden for the majority of the year.

Although this form of gardening is not without work, the results will be amply rewarding. Ring the changes with unusual and different combinations of plants to create displays which are both stunning as well as being intensely personal.

Vibrant Siberian wallflowers interplanted with scarlet tulips are one of the mainstays of this spring bedding scheme. Unusually plants have been arranged not just in blocks but in lines to give the effect of a piece of brightly printed fabric.

A glorious arrangement of summer bedding designed to arrest the eye. Here the owners of this small garden have mixed together marigolds, salvias and verbena edged with silver-leafed cineraria. This border will remain looking good until the frosts.

This somewhat uncompromising path leading to the front door of a modern house has been giving a daring, colourful treatment. Ribbons of shocking red salvias are interplanted with petunias in shades of magenta, pale mauve and pink. A small lawn on either side of the central path gives rest to the eye. Dwarf, slow growing conifers will, in future years, contribute height.

Tiny though this garden is, it has been given very definite character with this purposeful bedding scheme set out along formal lines. A limited variety of plants has been deliberately used in order to give a sense of unity.

Petunias are a marvellous standby and look so good when, as here, similar shades and tones are massed together. With all bedding plants, remember to feed routinely and to water plants when young as well as during periods of dry weather.

# A Garden of Perennials

Many gardeners, usually because of a lack of time, do not want to be bothered with constantly arranging and rearranging their gardens, often two or three times a year, with annuals, biennials or half hardy plants. For them the answer lies in a garden of perennials where effects, even if varying from season to season, will be constant from one year's end to the next.

Trees, shrubs and herbaceous perennials all fit this category and will, if sensibly chosen, and given time to establish, provide year-round interest and demand the minimum of maintenance. Periodically, of course, shrubs and trees may require some form of pruning, as indeed flowering perennials will eventually become overcrowded and need to be lifted and divided. But in the main work may be regulated to fit in with the individual's life style whilst ensuring a permanent display of interesting shape, form and colour.

This corner of 'A Concealed Garden' (see page 108) demonstrates how perennial plantings may reduce work to an absolute minimum. Closely planted bugle carpets the ground and effectively smothers weeds whilst the striking leaves of the hosta introduce variety of form.

Tightly clipped box cones underline the architectural quality which is the key-note of this particular garden. They successfully tie in with the yew hedging which forms a boundary.

Deep purple, silver and acidic green combine here to form a planting scheme which relies for its effect far more on foliage than on flower. Totally made up of perennials, this will have an attraction for the greater part of the year.

Beautifully colour co-ordinated and thoughtfully arranged herbaceous perennials mass this small border for maximum impact. The removal of faded flower heads helps to maintain the overall appearance and encourages further flowers.

Here the majority of space has been given over to the creation of a number of tiny borders, each one crammed with a colourful array of interesting and unusual perennials.

Granite sets, edged with stone, allow for access and reduce the necessity of treading on the ground when dead-heading. Most of these plants will be cut back close to ground level in the autumn.

# The Cottage Garden Look

Cottage gardens are never out of fashion. Perhaps deep down everyone's ideal is to garden in the deepest countryside surrounded by a medley of old fashioned flowers, home grown produce, meandering streams and sun-dappled grass. It is, therefore, hardly surprising that there is, in cities, suburbs and rural areas alike, so much interest in the cottage garden look.

Difficult to pin-point exactly, it is as much to do with atmosphere as arrangement, with feeling as with foliage and flower, and is certainly more to do with the casual than the contrived. The cottage garden is that wonderful mix of artfully placed perennials, of self-seeded annuals, of precious alpines, of herbs and vegetables all jostling for position and place.

A small garden is no bar to the cottage garden look. Even within a quite tiny space it is still possible to create the kind of delightful chaotic profusion which is so much admired. Well chosen perennials, a scattering of annual seed, scented shrubs, perhaps a miniature pond, and you should achieve a garden which not only recalls those of earlier times but which rapidly becomes a haven from the modern world.

A lovely arrangement of herbaceous perennials where a similar tone is used in a wide range of colour. Self-sown foxgloves, *Digitalis purpurea*, intermingle with the scabious-like *Knautia macedonica*. In the foreground the spherical head of the allium reflects the growth of the euphorbia.

This is very much in the tradition of the cottage garden where flower mixes with fruit, in this case a deep burgundy penstemon with ripening gooseberries.

An enchanting border mixture made up of a deep pink rose, a similar coloured diascia and all surrounded by a carpet of the white viola, *Viola cornuta alba*. Soon to flower are tall stemmed alliums with, almost certainly, purple-pink heads. This is cottage gardening with subtle sophistication which in no way detracts from its original purpose.

# Small City Gardens

If, as many of us do, you live in a large town or city, then it is very unlikely that you will have much space for a garden of any size. Indeed, you may well be restricted to a single window box, hanging baskets, or a few pots grouped around the entrance door. Whatever, it is still possible to create something of interest, to make a statement which, whilst being appropriate to the immediate environment, reflects your own personality and gardening style.

In the main, the smaller the area the simpler the basic idea should be. More of less works well in most garden situations and, when applied to tiny spaces, some stunning effects may be achieved. Form and texture may well be as important as colour which, for the most part, is seasonal and not always easy to maintain. Green, as a colour, is important in a heavily built-up area for it is suggestive of the countryside which lies beyond the town. An emphasis on foliage plants underlines the idea that the country is close by.

Much of the appeal of this city front garden lies in the fact that it has been planted for year-round interest. Evergreens, such as elaeagnus, skimmia and aucuba, ensure that there is something to look at even in the depths of winter.

By making a conscious decision to leave the central paved area free of planting, even to the extent of banishing pots, a splendid feeling of space is achieved.

The simple, quiet charm of this small court is maintained by dense plantings of evergreen shrubs and climbers. A single urn, topped with Universal pansies, heralds the onset of spring.

An unusual boat-shaped border in which colour is mainly limited to white with an accent of blue. Note how the extensive use of clipped box gives form to the whole, and is repeated in the stylish window boxes.

Evergreens, principally in tones of silver and green, make a welcoming statement at the entrance to this town house. Ivy, permitted to creep through the railings, softens any hard edges.

*Magnolia* 'Leonard Messel' flanked by scented choisya are the key plantings in this easily maintained, paved court. Both shrubs will continue to look attractive long after the flowers are over.

# The Kitchen Garden

A lack of space should not deter you from growing your own vegetables and herbs. It is perfectly true that produce freshly picked from the garden tastes better than anything that may be bought from a shop. That apart, there is immense satisfaction in preparing and then eating something which you have grown yourelf.

Where space is at a real premium, then establish a kitchen garden in a series of pots. It is quite surprising the number of vegetables which may be grown successfully under these conditions. Herbs, too, thrive in containers and may even be kept in the light on a kitchen window sill.

Vegetables and herbs do not have to be relegated to plots away from the flower garden. Many are not without decorative qualities and may be fitted snugly amongst shrubs and perennials where they will mature in an unobtrusive manner. Indeed, many traditional herbs are grown in mixed borders as a matter of course. Runner beans, always a favourite, take up very little space when grown up a wigwam sited at the back of the border. Try mixing them with midsummer daisies where their scarlet flowers will add additional colour.

Even the smallest of kitchen gardens can be exceedingly productive when crops are planted closely. Varieties requiring longer in the ground may be infilled with short term salad crops whilst successional sowings will always avoid a glut.

The way to the back gate is set out with a pleasant mixture of herbs and perennial flowers. Chinese onions, marjoram, thyme, sage and mint are all but a short step from the kitchen door. A flowering rosemary tones with the wisteria trained against the garden wall.

A patterned pathway, made up of old bricks and cobbles, is very much in keeping with the random planting and ensures dry feet in wet weather.

This vegetable border has been subdivided into a number of tiny plots by a series of narrow brick paths. Each area may be serviced without stepping onto and compacting the ground. The rotation of crops becomes easy in this situation. Note how ruby chard is grown alongside cauliflowers. As these are harvested, ground becomes available for further plantings.

Neatly trimmed box hedges contain both vegetables and herbs in this decorative potager. Access is via small paths, one brick in width, which follow the line of the hedges. Within each bed are crammed many different crop varieties. Inevitably the overall ordered effect is reduced somewhat once harvesting starts. At the rear of the garden panels of trellis conceal a working area.

As so many dishes make use of onions it makes good sense to grow your own. Although a long term crop, raised from seed or sets, they take up little room in the garden and are not unattractive in appearance. Once harvested they may be stored in a cool, dry place for a long period. This small onion bed is also home to the self-seeding *Viola labradorica*.

The foliage of the onions above has been turned over to expose them to the sun. Soon they will be ready to lift, dry off and store.

This little, neatly edged plot of lettuces would not look out of place anywhere. Easily grown from seed, lettuces will reach maturity within a few weeks. Different varieties have been included here to make summer salads both colourful and interesting. Over winter this same bed may be used for a longer term crop.

In order to keep the soil fertile it will be necessary to replenish it with well rotted compost, or any other organic matter, from time to time.

Asparagus is an absolute luxury, seldom readily available and always expensive. For these reasons it is certainly worth cultivating your own bed. Asparagus crowns, purchased and planted out in spring, require a sunny position in humus rich soil which is well drained.

Cropping should not begin until plants are at least three years old.

In this instance the asparagus has been interplanted with lettuces to maximize space.

*49*

Home grown early potatoes are one of the culinary delights of the onset of summer. That wonderful, earthy taste is somehow never present in those bought from a greengrocer or supermarket. Potatoes need not take up much space. It is possible simply to plant a couple of tubers, concealed somewhere at the back of the border, to enjoy a very satisfying crop. If space permits a compost heap, then try planting some potatoes in the rotting waste. They will certainly thrive. Even an old bucket, given drainage holes, will produce more than satisfactory results.

Carrots, peas, radishes, spinach, spring onions and sweet corn are all very easy vegetables to grow, are decorative in appearance and, most importantly, utilize little in the way of garden space. Each, too, has the further merit of reaching maturity in a relatively short period of time. Because of this valuable ground is not occupied for too long. Similarly vegetables such as broad beans, celery and leeks do not occupy too much space.

Where room is very limited, then it is probably best to avoid growing crops such as Brussel sprouts, cabbages and parsnips. All of these take up a great deal of ground, are not that pleasing to look at and are in situ for many months of the year.

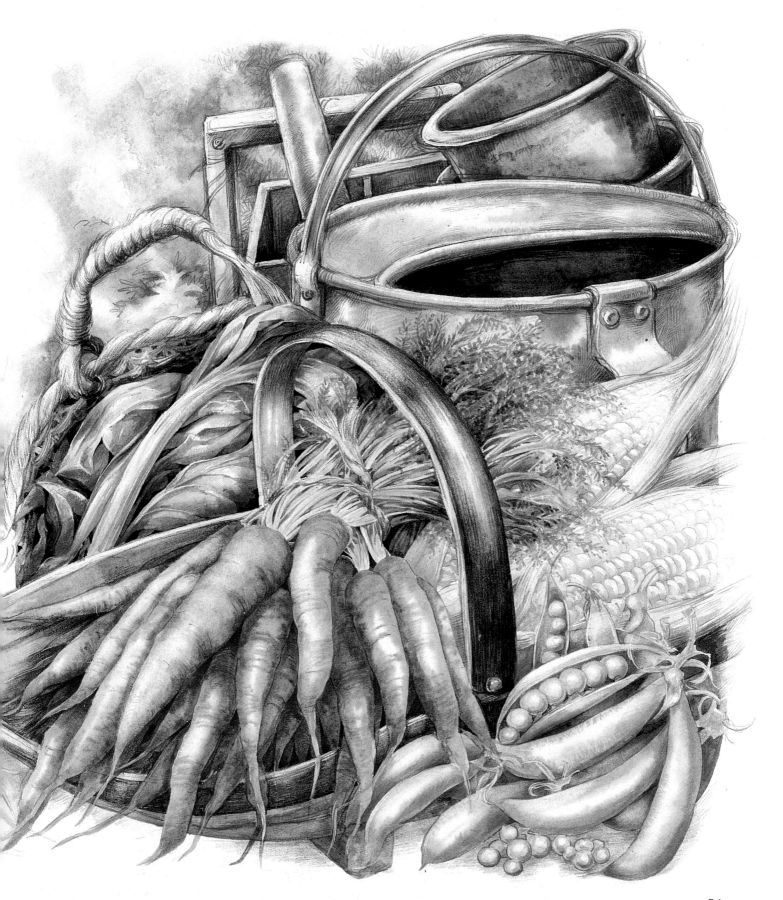

Anyone could adopt this splendid, original idea for growing courgettes. Here a large pot has been given good drainage, filled with fertile soil, planted out and placed in an old chimney pot. Surrounded with pineapple mint, whose leaves pick up the yellow of the courgette flower, it becomes part of a much larger composition.

Tomatoes taken straight from the garden are absolutely delicious to eat. No comparison can, or should, be made with those tasteless fruits which line so many of today's supermarket shelves.

Outdoor tomatoes may easily be grown, as here, in a pot. A sturdy cane to support the trusses, a position in full sun to assist ripening and plenty of water will result in excellent crops. Alternatively they may be cultivated in bags containing an appropriate growing medium. Such bags are sold at most garden centres.

Daily watering should, ideally, be supplemented once a week with a liquid tomato feed. Any fruits that remain green by the end of the summer may be ripened on a sunny window sill.

This vegetable plot is so small that even the wheelbarrow has been put to use as a container for the cultivation of courgettes. An original idea such as this will work perfectly well providing that adequate drainage is given. In hot, dry weather it may be necessary to water twice daily.

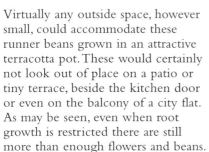

Virtually any outside space, however small, could accommodate these runner beans grown in an attractive terracotta pot. These would certainly not look out of place on a patio or tiny terrace, beside the kitchen door or even on the balcony of a city flat. As may be seen, even when root growth is restricted there are still more than enough flowers and beans.

Always remember when positioning any container to bear in mind its potential weight when the soil or compost is thoroughly wet.

Ginger mint, *Mentha* x *gentilis*, is fun to grow as an extra special ingredient in a mixed salad dressed with olive oil, vinegar and honey. Alternatively, finely chop the leaf-tips as an edible decoration for food.

A good sized pot, such as this attractive terracotta herb pot, may be planted up with a selection of culinary herbs chosen for their appealing foliage as well as their contribution to the kitchen.

Humus rich compost, to which is added a good handful of grit for drainage, is ideal for the mixed herbs which have been included here. Standing within reach of the kitchen door, where it is handy for watering purposes, this pot makes both a decorative and practical feature.

A nicely shaped rosemary and parsley, chives, oregano, French tarragon, winter savory and sage are all suitable for inclusion.

Garden mint, lovely for freshly made mint sauce and jelly, is kept within bounds by being planted in a pot which forms part of the overall display in this small potager. A container of mint could, very easily, be housed on a light kitchen window sill.

The whole of this very flourishing herb garden which, amazingly, is entirely contained within a series of pots, occupies very little space indeed. Rough sawn logs are used to form a rustic edging and the whole is set out on an area of gravel. Simple to create, this idea could readily be adapted to almost any situation.

One practical aspect of this kind of arrangement is that as plants go over the pots may be removed and replaced with something new and fresh.

There is nothing very sophisticated about this old enamel basin in itself, but once filled with a selection of carefully chosen herbs it takes on a new lease of life. Given a layer of crocks above drainage holes, easily drilled into the base, there is no reason at all why almost any container should not be transformed into a miniature herb garden.

Gone are the days when to grow apples and pears meant owning a garden of sufficient size to accommodate large, spreading, probably gnarled, fruit trees. With the introduction in recent years of dwarfing and semi-dwarfing rootstocks, it has become increasingly possible for every gardener to enjoy the pleasurable experience of plucking ripe fruit straight from the tree.

Where space is very much at a premium, then fruit trees may be trained against walls, fences or on wires in the form of cordons, espaliers or fans. Of course these methods all do demand careful pruning carried out at the correct time of year.

In situations where there is only room for a single tree, then it must, naturally, be a self-fertile variety. Specialist nurseries will be able to give advice in this respect.

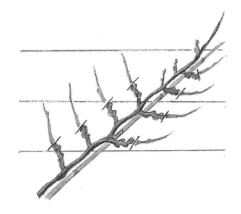

### FORMING A CORDON

A cordon of apples or pears becomes a very pleasing feature in any garden. Following the planting of a feathered maiden, reduce all sideshoots over 10cm/4in long to three buds. The leader should remain unpruned.

Step-over apples, like these, are an excellent answer to the problem of growing fruit in a very small garden. Planted along the edge of a border, or at the side of a path, they in time form an unusual and productive division.

The time to begin summer pruning of established cordons is once shoots have developed woody bases. Then shorten laterals back to three leaves beyond the basal cluster and cut back sub-laterals to one leaf beyond the basal cluster. When the leader reaches the required height, shorten it back to 15cm/6in above the top wire.

## FORMING AN ESPALIER

1. Prune a maiden tree back to a good bud 5cm/2in above the first wire.

2. In summer train the leading shoot to a cane as it develops. Train two side branches to canes at an angle of 45°. Shorten any other sideshoots to three leaves.

A somewhat plain brick wall has been transformed by this well-established espalier apple tree. During the mid to late summer laterals should be shortened back to three leaves and sub-laterals to one.

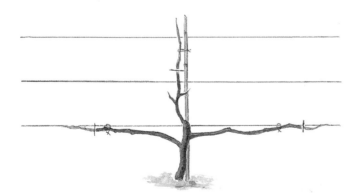

3. In late autumn tie down the arms of the first tier. Prune the leader to a bud, just above the second wire. Shorten other sideshoots to three buds.

4. In the second summer train the leader vertically and the two lateral branches at 45°. Shorten all other sideshoots to three leaves. Repeat this method until the required number of tiers has been formed. Prune back the leader in winter to just above the top tier.

Gooseberries need not, as might previously be thought, only be grown on bushes. In this imaginative scheme they have been trained along wires fixed to the house wall where, in full sunshine, they crop well. By training them in this way picking is made easy and sharp thorns are avoided. Gooseberries prefer soil which is slightly acidic.

This gooseberry bush has been grown as a standard to form a centrepiece to one of the sections of this box-edged kitchen garden. Much fun may be had by experimenting with growing familiar plants in different ways, often to achieve most original and pleasing effects.

Grapevines are, it is true, vigorous growers and will, in a normal situation, take up a great deal of space and certainly more than can be afforded in the small garden. However, with strict training they may be grown as cordons or espaliers or accommodated over arbours, arches or pergolas. It may be advisable to check before you buy that they will grow on your soil in your district.

Soft fruit in season is delicious and one of the pleasures of summer is to enjoy a bowl of freshly picked strawberries for supper. A strawberry jar, such as this handsome terracotta one, will allow fruit to develop without the risk of becoming muddied by earth. Place in full sun and keep well watered for fruit to ripen.

Currants are an essential ingredient of summer's feast and are lovely to include in all manner of puddings, not least the truly mouth watering summer pudding. Bushes need not be confined to particular areas for they merge quite happily into mixed borders.

# Selected Gardens

Small gardens and small spaces within larger gardens can take many forms. The gardens in this section are very individual. Some require a high degree of maintenance, others comparatively little; some are very colourful, others rely more on shape and texture for their appeal. Each is full of ideas that can be adapted to suit your requirements and tastes.

# A Garden Writer's Garden

Mirabel Osler's town garden, measuring little more than 21 x 9m/70 x 30ft, is a garden of extraordinary style. Here is the designer, the artist, the plantsperson in one, working with determination and confidence, with flair and artistry to create a garden which is innovative, inspiring and totally unexpected.

Underlying the whole garden is a strong framework of walls, paths, steps, interesting structures, unusual topiary, strategically placed containers and seats. Against this background is a wealth of planting where great emphasis is placed on foliage rather than flower. Colour, beyond all shades and tones of green, is deliberately restricted and controlled, thus when it does appear it is with even greater impact than might otherwise be the case.

Everywhere space is used in a thoughtful and imaginative manner. This is illustrated in the ways in which the boundaries have been completely concealed, utilities, such as a potting shed, accommodated, a water feature included, and a number of tiny but distinctly separate enclosures, each serving a definite purpose, have been woven into the whole.

Much of the charm of this very personal garden may be derived from a series of original touches. Concealed mirrors not only reflect light but suggest the surreal. Coloured gravel forms rivers of stone following a course amongst exuberant plantings. Modern sculpture harmonizes with antique pots and always there is a contrast of light and shadow, of space filled and of emptiness.

A solitary chair captures the sun's rays and invites a moment's pause and reflection. Although very much a town garden, there is a wonderful sense of privacy, of the world at a distance, of harmony with nature. Aromatic herbs and scented roses give to this sunny court a special appeal.

Framed by a plain but attractive wooden arch (opposite), a stone and brick path, the principal axis of the garden, draws the eye towards the distant boundary where a door, set in the wall, invites exploration of the beyond. That the door is false, and leads to nowhere, simply serves to highlight the imaginative detail which is to be found throughout this garden. A nice touch is the way in which at the lower level of the path the diamond shapes are of stone on brick. This pattern is reversed up the steps.

A beautifully planned sitting out area for summer meals. Clipped box encloses this outdoor room whilst *Salix caprea* 'Kilmarnock', the Kilmarnock willow, has, unusually, been shaped into lollipops. In the foreground a eucalyptus receives regular pollarding to control its size and to encourage blue growth. Behind the bench seat mirrors are placed; these effectively give an illusion of space. Weathered paving is in keeping with the overall simplicity and picks up on the plain, functional table and chairs.

A raised border gives necessary drainage to a collection of sun-loving plants, amongst which helianthemum (rock roses) are encouraged to tumble down the face of the stone wall. To the right the path leads through close plantings to the potting shed, itself playing host to a montana clematis. An Irish yew provides a vertical accent. By packing plants closely together a well-furnished look is achieved.

Within the gravel garden a sculpted slate urn is the dominant feature. Once more a mirror is used for an on-going reflection. Here the fastigiate yew is employed as a support for a climbing rose whose twining stems, ingeniously, assist in keeping the evergreen in shape. To the right of the picture *Viburnum plicatum* 'Mariesii' flowers profusely. This shrub, along with others, is kept in bounds with judicious pruning.

This little water feature has, in fact, a practical purpose. As a dipping well, topped up by the adjacent tap, it is conveniently placed to sink a can for a ready supply of sun-warmed water for summer watering.

Placed where it may be reflected in a mirror, a wicker basket for the collection of prunings and other garden waste takes on a secondary rôle as a focal point. By raising it off the ground, wet rot is avoided.

These few shallow steps leading to the false door terminate a main vista. A pair of empty urns, in stark contrast to the profusion of planting all around, contribute symmetry as well as seeming to exercise a control over nature.

Trapped by the heat of the sun, this generous grouping of pots conjures up the spirit of the Mediterranean. Cranesbill, lilies and violas ensure colour and interest over a long period.

Returning to the house, attention focuses on an arrangement of pots placed beside the open door. The textured surface of the path guards against slipping in wet weather whilst plants are encouraged to spill over from the borders.

Incredibly this charming summerhouse is tucked away into a tiny space just off the main path. Carefully sited, it is positioned to look directly across the gravel garden where, artfully, a visual colour link is made.

Paint is important in this garden. Here the exterior of the summerhouse is painted grey-blue with details picked out in grey-green. Within, a bench seat, useful for storage purposes, is coloured a wonderful, distressed chalk-blue, a colour repeated on some of the wood panels behind. These in turn are set off with alternate panels of pale terracotta. Cushions, of similar tones, are casually strewn to introduce a touch of relaxed informality. Framed paintings suggest this is a room to be lived in, an extension of the house.

Detail is closely observed. The pleasing line of the roof reflects that of the doorway. Carving on the back of the bench is not dissimilar to that used between the front supporting pillars. Stone chosen for the floor has, almost certainly, inspired the choice of colour for paint.

Behind the summerhouse, and continuing along the wall at either side, trellis of a similar colour has been used to give added height. Not only does this ensure greater privacy but does, of course, open up an additional area where plants may be trained. Roses, seen here, will at the height of the season completely mask the support.

Gardens are, very naturally, not only places in which to work but are also, as indicated here, places of leisure. Ample seating, both outside and under cover, provision for outdoor eating as well as strategically sited resting points contribute to an atmosphere of carefree relaxation which is very much the essence and spirit of this garden.

## An Award Winning Small Garden

Considerable skill and ingenuity on the owners' part have gone into the creation and maintenance of this colourful edge-of-town garden. Given the fact that it is designed to provide colour from early spring right through until the frosts of autumn, it is of no surprise that it was selected as best small garden in a national magazine.

What is incredible, and wholly impressive, is that the vast majority of all the plants are raised by the owners in their small, standard greenhouse which, later in the year, becomes a principal attraction in its own right. And, not content with a few varieties, the range of plants grown guarantees that any visitor to the garden will, almost certainly, encounter new delights previously unknown.

Early spring and the greenhouse is just getting under way. Young seedlings, neatly pricked out, are starting to take root, the first of many. Bubble wrap around the glass helps to maintain an even temperature.

Cheerful daffodils, polyanthus and yellow-flowered forsythia contribute early spring colour and hint at what is to come. Grown in pots, which could very easily be sunk into the ground, these bulbs will later be stored out of the way.

Cold frames, seen in the foreground, are already fully utilized with stock being brought on for the main flowering season which, pictured right, occurs in summertime.

By early summer the garden is taking on a very different appearance. Both borders and pots are starting to burgeon and, with the absence of frosts, half-hardy annuals may be set out in position.

Compared with the start of the gardening year, the greenhouse is set to come into its own. No longer a place for the raising of seeds and the nurturing of cuttings, it now takes pride of place.

Herbaceous perennials cram the border which runs the length of one side of the garden. Here are to be found all the old favourites – lupins, delphiniums, clematis, roses, lilies and scarlet *Lychnis chalcedonica*.

Midsummer and the garden is a riot of many splendid hues, each jostling for position and attention. All the hard work, and no little anxiety, of the early year come to fruition in this cavalcade of colour.

Undoubtedly one of the secrets of success is to position plants as closely together as possible. Here no bare earth is allowed to be seen, nor can there be even the hint of a gap between pots.

By now the interior of the greenhouse is full to bursting point leaving precious little room for regular watering and feeding which are so necessary if plants like these are to flourish.

Staging, arranged in tiers, is essential to display this many plants to such good effect. Careful, secure positioning of pots is very much part of the routine work of the garden.

Large numbers of the plants used in the summer displays, such as these elegant fuchsias, are not able to withstand low winter temperatures. Protection from frost, in a heated greenhouse, is essential for their survival.

A dark green conifer hedge serves not only to give privacy to the garden but as an excellent, plain foil to the many coloured plants.

Fuchsias, some tender, some hardy, are amongst the mainstays of the summer bedding. Here tones of pink and purple harmonize together in this section of the border.

Bright heads of begonias provide startling colour as the season progresses. These are in fact grown in a narrow space alongside the greenhouse, fully illustrating the point that nowhere is left bare.

A narrow bed against the garage wall is home to massed planting. Edging the grass is a row of pink and red pelargoniums, their felted, marked leaves providing additional interest.

Fluttering above the border is the tiny Canary creeper whose harvest-yellow flowers show up against a dark-leafed background.

Planting in and around the patio makes use of soft pinks, white, violet-blue and deep purple. Staking, as the bamboo cane reveals, is necessary if taller growing plants are to remain upright.

A flourish of colour descends the house wall in the form of a swag of flowers. This attractive display makes artful use of a series of pots, each one carefully secured to the brick.

# *A Family Town Garden*

A grass path of generous proportions runs from the house to the far boundary. On either side mellow brick walls give shelter to an attractive mix of old-fashioned and much loved plants. A nesting box, shown on the far left, is a source of fascination for grandchildren.

Creating a garden which is, on the one hand, inviting and accessible to young children and, on the other, retains a sense of order and purpose, and is in itself a visual delight, is no easy matter. But that is exactly what has been achieved in this stylish small garden which lies behind a Georgian town house.

For the gardener, this is a flower garden of the utmost charm. Traditional borders of trees, shrubs and herbaceous perennials are combined with a sunny terraced area, shady corner and pleasant places for sitting. For children it becomes an adventure playground with space for ball games, nooks and crannies in which to hide and, best of all, a magnificent tree house.

That apart, what this garden clearly demonstrates is that it is not necessary to divide an area, with walls, trellis, hedges or shrubs, in order to create very distinct, quite separate spaces for working, playing or, simply, relaxing.

Surrounded by self-seeded foxgloves, this bench seat is a pleasant place in which to absorb the sights, sounds and scents of the garden. Pots give added interest and are moved around as the season advances. Brick underfoot ties in with the wall and keeps feet dry in wet weather.

What child could resist the thrill of this proper tree house? Purpose built, and approached by a stout ladder, this is something straight from the pages of Peter Pan. And, one suspects, it is not just children who climb up to enter a world of the imagination, of fantasy and excitement. Although this is intended very naturally for children it does, notwithstanding, blend sympathetically into the garden. Wind chimes add a special touch.

This corner of a border (left) conveys a wonderful sense of plants in profusion. Here are to be found everyone's favourites set out in daring abandon. Delphiniums, lupins, columbines and forget-me-nots are joined by cistus, irises and roses. This is the cottage garden of the past reborn into the town. Such informality reflects very much the gardening style of the owners. In this garden annuals and perennials are encouraged to seed around. Control, in the form of tying-in and staking, is kept to a minimum. In short, plants are given free-reign and they respond well.

In direct contrast to the more open borders, this area of shade captures an entirely different mood. Greater emphasis is placed on foliage and form, less on colour. Here is something altogether quieter, more subdued, a retreat from the bright sunlight which floods the other end of the garden.

With this in mind a second outdoor eating area has been created amongst all this lush canopy of leaves. Against the wall, framed by a metal arch, a bearded face solemnly surveys the scene.

A brick terrace running alongside the house ends in a plethora of foliage. Much thought has been given to the placing of different shrubs, grasses and ferns to create a tapestry of green. Leaf shape plays an important part in this grouping which is never allowed to look dull or repetitive. A creeper (*Parthenocissus henryana*) carries the theme to the wall of the house.

Summer meals are enjoyed in this sunny, open-air dining area which, situated close to the back door, is convenient for the kitchen. On the wall an arrangement of ceramic tiles forms an outdoor picture. Much use has been made of the lovely, old brick garden walls as a permanent support for climbers. Ivy is included but is never allowed to get out of hand.

## A Garden Designer's Garden

Jacquie Gordon, a garden designer, was faced with the challenge of creating a private space within an area overlooked by a new housing development. One of the main priorities was, understandably, to provide complete seclusion yet maintain a degree of openness essential if the garden was not to feel claustrophobic.

As someone with a demanding career, consideration needed to be given to the amount of time available for maintenance. If the garden were to fit in with a busy lifestyle, then it had to be capable for the most part of looking after itself. Finally, at the end of a hectic day the garden should provide a refuge from work, a welcoming environment in which to potter and relax.

All of this, and much more, has been achieved with an apparent ease which belies clear-sighted ideas, rigorous planning, firm discipline, and bold realization.

The garden as it was. An ugly fence, barely concealed, the windows of neighbouring houses and, on the left, the rampant Russian vine, *Polygonum baldschuanicum*. Even at this stage plans are being formulated as boards and canes set out on the grass testify.

Contrasts of form and texture are the keynote here. A giant phormium, whose spiky leaves stab at the skyline, is balanced by a feathery acer. Underfoot gravel, brick and granite paviours complement each other. An interesting bamboo screen makes an architectural boundary.

It is scarcely possible that this (see opposite) is the same garden. No longer overlooked, unsightly fencing obliterated, the Russian vine ripped out, all to be replaced by a tapestry of plants, thoughtfully positioned hard landscaping and a seemingly casual arrangement of pots and containers. Much skill lies in the design where, even in what is no more than a smallish square, it has been possible to suggest a garden of much greater size.

Blocking out a view which lacks interest, this planting of trees adds necessary height and, skilfully, depth to the end of the garden. Care has been taken to choose trees whose canopy will not become too dense.

This grouping of pots, almost a pot garden in itself, brings colour and interest to this corner of the garden. Such an arrangement allows great flexibility; as plants peak so they may be brought into prominence and then 'retired' once their flowering season is past.

No garden should be without a seating area. Here daring paint colours of slate-blue and fabrics of cerise pink have been used to great effect against a background made up principally of green and gold foliage plants. The chair, placed to one side, invites conversation.

A bird's eye view of the entire garden. From the vantage point of an upstairs window it is possible to appreciate fully the design, structure and plantings of this most intriguing garden.

Circles, suggested in the pool, the many plant containers and the shape of the border, are in marked contrast to the angular paving, the bamboo screen, even the bench. Vertical accents are reinforced by the trunks of the trees, tall growing perennials, among them stately euphorbias, and the old chimney pot, now invested with a new lease of life as a plant pot holder.

Colour plays an important part in the overall design of the garden. Grey and silver leafed plants thread through the borders, cooling down hot splashes of gold. Of these, most notable are artemisia, eucalyptus, euonymus, and the pampas grass, *Cortaderia selloana*. Blue is continuously hinted at and is to be found not only in flower colour but repeated in blue pots, blue cushions and in the colour of the seat.

Brimming with design ideas, this small garden illustrates how a somewhat uninspiring, conventional plot may be transformed into an imaginative, highly individual and personal area to provide enjoyment, interest and colour throughout each season of the year.

# A Plant Lover's Garden

In dividing up a fairly typical back garden in a leafy suburb of a small cathedral city, the owners deliberately set out to create two very distinct and special areas for their growing collection of rare and beautiful plants. Neither space is at all large, but this has proved no barrier to creating borders designed for year-round interest. In addition to permanent plantings of trees, shrubs and perennials, much use is made of half-hardy subjects which, overwintered in a frost free greenhouse, are introduced into the borders at flowering time.

Gardening in this way is both time consuming and labour intensive. Spring flowering bulbs are removed as they go over, their spaces filled with unusual summer bedding. Perennials, if they are to be kept in peak condition, must be lifted and divided on a regular basis. Excessive growth on trees and shrubs is constantly checked to maintain a correct balance within borders. Climbers are tied-in and trained in accordance with a master plan. All of this beside the routine tasks of dead-heading, of lawn care, of weeding and feeding, of mulching and, when necessary, watering.

A passion for plants has not, as is sometimes the case, resulted in random and restless plantings. Borders are very carefully and thoughtfully co-ordinated with a keen eye for detail. Colour combinations, an awareness of form and texture and an appreciation of the finer points all contribute towards a satisfying whole.

Pastel shades of early summer dominate a well structured herbaceous border. Close planting not only ensures that a maximum number of plants may be fitted into a small space, but minimises the need for staking. Tall growing perennials are arranged in such a way as to support and be supported by their neighbours.

A trellis divides this border from the white garden which lies immediately behind. An open structure like this allows the free circulation of air and light.

Majestic delphiniums, Pacific Hybrids, contrast wonderfully with a deep background of a plum coloured prunus. Cut down once the flower spires are finished, they will in all probability reward with a repeat flowering. Interest is sustained with the inclusion of the magenta flowered cranesbill, *Geranium psilostemon*, and blood-red peonies. Later, tender lobelias and salvias will be added to sustain the border right through until the first frosts of autumn.

Parallel herbaceous borders in the grand manner have been adapted to a small space. Linked by similar but not identical plantings, they terminate in an inviting arbour wreathed in honeysuckle, *Lonicera × americana*, and the sweetly scented rose, *Rosa* 'New Dawn'. Although the garden contains a large number of very unusual plants, the owners have not dismissed easy, all time favourites. Much use is made of catmint, *Nepeta* 'Six Hills Giant', and lady's mantle, *Alchemilla mollis*. Planted at intervals along the length of both borders, they create a sense of pattern and give a feeling of continuity. Well tended, neatly edged grass sets off the whole.

A paved path (left), provides a colourful link between the two garden areas. Pots of white marguerites, beautifully cool and summery, unify both sides. In the foreground the half-hardy geranium, *Geranium malviflorum*, sprays out onto the flags.

From the seat in the arbour the vista is closed by this formal arrangement set before a tightly clipped privet hedge. Shaped box, grown in sturdy terracotta pots, guard a handsome plinth and ball made from salvaged materials. Scrambling over this is the pale pink *Clematis* 'Betty Corning', a cross between *C. viticella* and *C. texensis*.

Surrounding the plinth (right) is a massed planting of the crimson thistle, *Cirsium rivulare* 'Atropurpureum'. This perennial requires an open, sunny spot where it will flower for many weeks on end. Once the flowers are over, the finely cut foliage remains as a contrast to the leaves of nearby clematis and privet.

Throughout the garden the owners' policy is intentionally to plant in groups of one kind, thus avoiding the fussiness that single plants can so often give.

Rain contributes a soft, slightly melancholy air to this approach to the white garden. Across the rose arch, *Rosa* 'Albéric Barbier' and *Rosa* 'Alister Stella Gray' tussle for position. The blue of a eucalyptus is picked up by a grass of similar tone, an introduction which disallows any monotony which might be brought about by a single colour. A second pair of clipped box trees, recalling those of the previous garden, help to frame the view.

Gravel, at the centre of which a stone bird bath forms a focal point, encourages self-seeding which contributes an air of relaxation in an otherwise formal setting. Tall flowering verbascums are matched with elegant campanulas, sibirica irises, scented dianthus and sprawling cranesbill.

Density of planting ensures that this garden maintains a feeling of secrecy, well shut off from neighbouring properties and nearby city life.

One of the main achievements of this garden comes from the way in which the owners have handled changes of direction and mood. Movement from one area to another, from one colour scheme to another, is gradual and, for the most part, barely perceptible. Here cool whites are replaced with soft pinky-white, pale blues with stronger violet-blues. And, as elsewhere, green foliage provides a constant background.

# A Green Town Garden

Few, if any, could fail to be captivated by the utter charm of this, the most delightful of tiny, tiny town gardens. Approached from the busy street through a handsome brick arch, this oasis of green offers a haven of order, peace and tranquillity in direct contrast to the commotion of modern day life to be found outside its walls.

In describing it as a green garden is not, of course, to suggest that all plantings are restricted to this one colour. Far from it. But what the owners have done in the first instance is to build up a background and structure of foliage plants, chosen for form and texture, against which to set off carefully selected flowering shrubs and perennials. Planting within a very small space demands great discipline for every plant must be worthy of inclusion and must work hard to earn its keep.

A garden such as this is not necessarily low on maintenance. Fewer flowers there may be, but a programme of regular pruning, training and trimming is required to ensure that nature is kept within bounds and that the overall effect of luxuriant planting is not lost nor allowed to get out of hand.

Undoubtedly the joy of this garden lies in the owners' personal vision. No garden should be slavishly copied and this one is no exception to that rule. However, what may be drawn from it is the certain knowledge that, no matter how small or unpromising, how unlikely the site may appear, every plot of ground of whatever description has potential, and that potential is there to be realized.

Looking from the street towards the house (above), the edges of the pathway are crammed with an exciting mixture of plants. Roses scramble among taller growing shrubs and trees whilst at ground level *Alchemilla mollis*, the lady's mantle, cavorts with other low-growing and ground-hugging perennials. Punctuating the path, and acting as sentinels, are a series of evergreen *Chamaecyparis lawsoniana* 'Columnaris', closely wired to maintain their shape.

The view (opposite) from the house. On the left a plinth of small leafed ivy is surmounted by a terracotta pot containing box which, in time, will be clipped to shape. Facing it, across the path, is a similar arrangement but this time the ivy is variegated, chosen to pick up the yellow of the hosta leaf. Midway towards the entrance the white bark of *Betula utilis* var. *jacquemontii* soars upwards.

From the conservatory a path, flanked by two splendid stone dogs, invites exploration of a second garden area. The way in which the path is designed to curve slightly has the effect of appearing to lengthen the distance as well as preventing the whole from being seen at a glance. Planting is wonderfully dense and varied, chosen to give depth and intensity to a small space. A number of different ivies used as ground cover also act to soften stone edges. Ferns with their shapely fronds contrast with the strap-like leaves of irises.

What impresses most about this garden is the total restraint which has been placed upon it in terms of planning and execution. Single ideas have been developed fully and deliberately in a situation where it would have been all too easy to have played with many. A nice balance has been struck between the formal and informality. And, so often overlooked, there is an obvious awareness of the importance of light and shade, of mass and void, of atmosphere and mood.

Raised beds have been used widely throughout this garden. Retaining stone walls have the effect of sinking paths to a lower level and allowing them to take on an intimacy otherwise denied. The inclusion of stone troughs and pots for alpines helps maximise all available space in addition to providing a visual link between path and border. Note the way in which cracks and crevices have become home to tiny self-seeders.

As the way gently curves to rejoin the path at the front of the house, so the eye is drawn once more to another quiet but inspiring planting scheme. Here green is highlighted with white. Tall growing white foxgloves, *Digitalis purpurea albiflora*, combine with the masterwort, *Astrantia major involucrata*, to float among a dappled canopy of leaves. Edging the front of the border, to give a sense of unity and purpose, is a ribbon of white-margined ivy.

Last, but by no means least, a single Ali Baba jar adds dignity to an otherwise forgotten corner.

# A Gravel Garden

A flight of stone steps leads from the house down into this gravel garden. Enclosed on all sides by high walls, the heat from the summer sun remains trapped so that the entire court, even in winter, enjoys a very favourable micro-climate. Mindful of this, the owners have consciously sought to create an area suitable for the cultivation of sun-loving plants.

A thick mulch of pea gravel acts as an irregular path through the garden. In practical terms this not only reflects the heat but also serves to conserve moisture. Additionally, of course, the gravel provides sun-loving plants with the sharp drainage that they require if they are to thrive.

Planting is very much colour-themed. Soft pinks, lilacs, lavenders and mauves are highlighted with a touch of crimson, isolated instances of indigo blue and splashes of palest lemon. Glaucous foliage, typical of plants capable of withstanding the hot sun, contributes to the overall effect. A changing display of pots guarantees that the garden is never static.

The casual elegance with which plants are set in the gravel, the way in which climbers effortlessly drape the walls and the inclusion of burgeoning pots suggests a garden of relatively easy maintenance. Unfortunately, this is not necessarily the case. Gravel demands regular raking, unwanted seedlings must be removed, pots require watering and climbers need to be trained. However, such work carried out on a regular basis will, almost certainly, result in a garden as attractive and pleasing as this one.

Lovely combinations such as this one may be achieved by pairing plants. By growing two climbers together not only are out-of-the-way effects achieved but it becomes possible to lengthen considerably the season of interest. Pictured here are *Wisteria floribunda* and *Clematis montana* 'Tetrarose'.

Finely divided leaves of *Choisya ternata* 'Aztec Pearl' give this form of the Mexican orange bush a particular appeal. Its sweetly scented flowers will be especially fragrant in this enclosed garden. Blue flower heads of a camassia complete the picture.

This splendid, glazed Ali Baba pot is home to a fine specimen of *Aeonium arboreum*. During winter months the tender aeonium is returned to the conservatory where it becomes an indoor feature.

*Dierama*, or angels' fishing rod, provides an excellent contrast of form. It enjoys the good drainage of the gravel garden and will, in most years, provide seedlings round and about.

Frequent pruning and the removal of unwanted suckers are necessary to check the growth of the grey-leafed sea buckthorn, *Hippophaë rhamnoïdes*, which the owners particularly wished to include as a foil to *Rosa* 'Cerise Bouquet' as well as other plantings.

Large clumps of the low-growing, pretty pink *Phuopsis stylosa* are encouraged to sprawl at the edge of the gravel walk where they are in flower for most of the summer. They help to give an air of informality.

All of the cistus love to be baked so their inclusion in this hot, dry garden is of little surprise. *Cistus* 'Elma', shown here, has been chosen for its large, papery-white petals surrounding a centre of golden stamens.

In the spring any frost damaged branches are removed and straggly growth shortened. Care is taken not to cut into old wood.

Successful colour combinations are one of the principal delights of this gravel garden. By keeping within broad bands of colour the owners have achieved a number of eye-catching and intensely pleasing plant associations.

Flowers of *Cistus* 'Peggy Sammons' intermingle in this particular scheme with the lilac trumpets of *Penstemon glaber*. Regular dead-heading of the penstemon keeps flower colour all summer long.

# Terracing a Hillside

Situated in an enviable position on the edge of a major city overlooking a deep gorge, the steepness of the site of this garden called for radical treatment. Julian Dowle, international garden designer, decided, in consultation with the owner, to reconstruct and redesign the series of small terraces linked by steps and meandering paths. Coupled with this he arranged for a number of formal and informal pools, connected by water courses and channels, to form a principal feature of the garden as a whole.

Considerable site excavation, with the aid of mechanical diggers, was necessary to establish levels and large quantities of stone imported for the construction of retaining walls. The installation of a complex water system demanded advanced technical knowledge not only of the management of water but also of electricity.

The result is a garden or, more accurately, several individual gardens, which have been designed to take full advantage of spectacular views, which harmonize with the surrounding landscape, and which are highly original in concept and execution.

Beyond the fine view, glimpsed through overgrown trees and shrubs, there is little to commend the garden as it was. Any planned development has to take account of the steeply sloping nature of the site.

Hard landscaping is in place and the garden is beginning to take shape. Clearly shown is the way in which the designer has overcome the problem of the slope with a series of linked terraces. Clearance has resulted in a broader view of the gorge.

Looking upwards towards the house the extent of the terracing is immediately apparent. At this stage planting is yet to be undertaken although, as may be seen, borders are freshly dug and manured. Drainage pipes, inserted into retaining walls, will help to carry away surplus rainwater. Although the site is steep, steps are shallow and placed at intervals to make for easy access.

Lush planting (below) successfully masks the somewhat stark edges of the hard landscaping and gives to the whole garden a slight air of mystery. Water, coursing from one level to another, beckons and reinforces a desire for exploration. Boundaries have been largely disguised with trees, shrubs and climbers. To the right of the picture the top of the gazebo is clearly visible.

An informally shaped pool is the dominant feature of this level. Close planting includes many moisture loving marginals, including a generous clump of the arum-like *Zantedeschia aethiopica*. The small stone channel carries water down to the next terrace.

The descent from the top terrace is via a series of steps and a stone bridge, placed as a crossing point over the narrow end of the pool. Extensive use is made of hostas and bergenias, their broad leaves associating well with water.

Contrasts of form and texture are achieved in this imaginative poolside planting. A damp spot has been found for the moisture loving *Primula vialii* with its distinctive cone-shaped red and lavender flowers.

One of the chief delights of these small terraces is the way in which it is possible to view the garden from different vantage points. Here you are able to be at eye-level with this pool of water. An utterly magical experience.

The gazebo sits snugly in the corner of two walls on this lower level. Sides are clothed with climbers whilst over the roof a rose is allowed to scramble unchecked. A structure such as this, which fits easily into a small space, serves not only as a sitting out place but also as a focal point.

Water, from an upper reach, cascades down this shute into a formal basin, its splashing sound enjoyed from the seat within the gazebo. Care has been taken not only to ensure that each area of the garden is not without interest, but that each has a distinctive mood and character.

An integral part of an ingenious water system, this lion mask spouts water downwards into the formal pool whilst the fountain returns it up. Solid supporting walls are clothed with a wisteria, below which irises enjoy a sun-baked position. Lavenders add their perfume to this scented garden.

A formal pool, complete with fountain, is the keynote of this lower terrace. A weathered seat proves a pleasant place in which to sit and enjoy both garden and view. Water lilies pick up the pink tones of neighbouring clematis and roses.

From the fountain garden the way descends to yet another level. Viewed from above, the planting is deliberately restricted so that foliage succeeds flower. Such a contrast brings with it a change of atmosphere and mood.

This quiet terrace acts as an interlude before the final way down. The spreading branches of an established lime tree gives a canopy of light shade and enhances a cool and restful scheme.

In a garden where space does not allow for a lawn, a plain, simply planted area is an important substitute.

The bottom pool, the final goal, is surrounded with dense plantings. Ferns, goat's beard (*Aruncus dioicus*), marsh marigolds, variegated irises and the paddle leaves of *Lysichiton camtschatcensis* all jostle for position. The inclusion of water here, at the lowest of levels, gives point and meaning to the whole of the water system which runs as a common theme throughout the garden.

A doorway, set into the stone wall, leads out of the garden and gives direct access to the gorge. In what is, after all, an enclosed garden it provides an important link with the world outside.

Not surprisingly this final garden includes a charming little summerhouse. This timber framed structure is very much in keeping with its less formal surroundings and provides a welcome resting place.

The scale of the terracing is quite daunting when viewed from the bottom level. However, cleverly designed breaks in the line, shown here in the gap in the wall and the archway, together with sympathetic plantings chosen to soften all hard edges, ensure that the stone is never allowed to overpower. The material of the gazebo, top left of the picture, is in direct contrast to the stone walling.

An overall view of the garden showing the way in which the separate parts contribute to the whole. Much of the success of this garden lies in a bold plan supported by well-defined structures against which is a profusion of planting.

The dramatic use of water, introduced at virtually every level, adds excitement and interest to a garden which is, in every respect, unique.

# An Enclosed Court

High hornbeam hedges completely enclose this small court tucked into a tiny space immediately outside the kitchen door. Old flagstones cover the ground upon which are set a selection of clay pots which are changed according to the season. Furnishings are deliberately kept simple – a painted bench and weathered table with the addition of an extra chair or two when visitors arrive.

For the owners this is a garden in which to relax, to entertain friends and to enjoy the occasional summer meal outside. Because of this low maintenance is a priority but at the same time there is a desire to be surrounded with interesting, unusual and attractive plants.

Scented lilies (see right) are a must for high summer and are especially good as pot specimens. Surrounding these are tender fuchsias, pelargoniums and well grown eucomis with deep green, strap-like leaves and amazing flower heads. Supported on the table is a splendid pot of asarina whose glaucous leaves arch gracefully downwards. Throughout the growing period plants are kept in good condition with slow release, organic fertilizer. Care is taken to ensure that regular watering takes place and that pots are never allowed to dry out.

A lovely combination of *Lilium* 'Pink Perfection', fuchsia and dainty nemesia. Once the lily is over, flower heads will be removed and the arrangement will remain pleasing for the rest of the summer.

Dark headed fuchsias are a perfect foil for the shell-pink bells of pot grown *Azorina vidalii*. In the background lilies are about to open into flower.

Wonderful waxy blooms of *Kirengeshoma palmata* are cultivated in a narrow border where they enjoy the partially shady situation. These later flowering perennials are not difficult to grow but should be given humus-rich soil which is kept moist during the flowering period.

Close to the kitchen door (left) is a fine example of the winter flowering *Garrya elliptica*. Long tassels make a striking feature during the dark days of winter and give life to the court during an otherwise dark season. Although garrya is capable of becoming a large shrub, regular pruning will keep it in trim and to size.

Clear pink blooms of *Camellia* 'Anticipation' are teamed up here with the darker tones of the spring flowering *Clematis alpina* 'Ruby'. In a small space it is fun to experiment to see how many different plants may be encouraged to work together.

Clipped box edges the borders which surround this courtyard garden (right). Not only does it serve to contain the plants but also introduces a note of formality which is very much in keeping with the situation. A shaped ball of box develops the theme as will the shapes positioned at intervals along the hedge when fully grown. Plumes of *Smilacina racemosa* complete the spring picture.

## A Concealed Garden

Nothing in the approach, through the sprawling suburbs of a large industrial city, prepares the visitor for the unique quality of this totally secret and superbly styled garden. Even with detailed directions to hand, when confronted with huge, painted galvanised gates, like those at the entrance to a factory, set on the boundary of an area of common land tucked behind a row of terraced houses, it is all too easy to believe that the whole thing is a mistake, that there can be little of worth there if, indeed, anything at all. But nothing is further from the truth. To pass through the formidable gates is to enter a world transformed. Gone is the bleakness of the outer suburbs to be replaced with a garden, though small in overall size, which has been cleverly crafted into a series of inter-connecting, individual outside rooms.

Immediately it is apparent that form and structure mean a great deal to the owners. Clipped yew hedging is used on a grand scale as the principal means of delineating enclosures. Box is fashioned in balls, cones, pyramids and spirals, or simply used as low divisions, to give unity, and a sense of fun, to individual areas. Recycled timbers, substantial in appearance, give substance to paths and steps, strongly countering any suggestion of the whimsy.

For although much use is made of flowering shrubs and perennials, this is not in essence a flower garden. The passion here is for symmetry, for proportion, shape and order. Each individual garden is planned in such a way as to connect with its neighbours so that it is possible to stand in one place and look first into one unfolding vista, then into another and another.

As busy professional people, the owners are able to give less time than they would like to garden maintenance. To this end the garden has been planned to survive and yet to look good for long periods of time. Outside work can be reduced to routine mowing of the small lawn, regular hedge trimming and the brushing of paths. These jobs complete, the garden conveys a wonderful sense of order and harmony, of being cared for and well loved.

A cross vista, terminating in a sculptural shell, is strongly defined with a series of box cones. Paths are of gravel contained within granite sets which are in keeping with an overall severity of style. Deep purple leaf tones of the ajuga, widely used on each corner as ground cover, echo the purplish-black hue of the mounted shell. Behind, a young yew hedge has yet to reach its ultimate height.

Bold steps framed with hefty wooden stumps are almost in themselves an item of sculpture. The uncompromising, rather masculine mood of the garden is softened with carefully thought out plantings. Here both ferns and lady's mantle succeed in breaking stark outlines. Changes of level throughout, at times artificially created, serve to heighten awareness and dispel any feeling of sameness.

This cross path, opening onto an expanse of grass, has been planned deliberately to be narrow in order to create spatial contrast. Granite sets, stone blocks, flagstones and old timbers make for interesting and varied hard landscaping.

Formal structures and informal plantings go hand in hand in this simple but effective area. Engineering blocks displayed in blue-grey gravel are contained within a solid wooden frame. A pair of stone vases contain a mixture of houseleeks.

Unashamedly theatrical, this dramatic flight of outdoor stairs rises towards a stark, elemental sculpture. At intervals the yew is cut to give glimpses, and sometimes access, into the 'wings'. Mindful of proportion and scale this becomes, rightly, a tour de force.

Tightly clipped box balls demonstrate the importance that the owners of this garden give to form. A nice touch has been to imitate the shape of the box with the heads of ornamental onions, just now going to seed.

Two openings, one at either side of this border, give access to a further garden area which will, as the yew continues to develop, become completely concealed.

Framed on all sides by hedges of yew, this boldly painted seat acts both as a focal point to end a vista and also as a resting place. Yet again, as elsewhere in this garden, materials for paths are varied and employed in an imaginative manner.

House colours are applied in this situation where the bench seat becomes part of a much larger composition. Climbers, trained up the obelisks, are never allowed to mask their structure. Clumps of bergenia point the direction of the path out of this particular area.

One of the underlying strengths of this garden is the way in which the owners have contrived a series of vistas whereby it is possible to look from one enclosure into another. This tiny silver and white garden is approached from four directions.

In order for it to be effective, and especially so in a very small space, box hedging must be kept crisply cut at all times. The vista in this direction opens onto the courtyard surrounding the studio.

This side of the silver and white garden is dominated by a summerhouse faced in dressed stone. The interior walls are painted a deep terracotta red and decorated with carved swags. Lilies, presently in bud, will drown the air with their heady scent.

The fourth approach, as seen from the summerhouse, takes good account of perspective. The alteration in the levels arrests the eye and places the whole scene into slow motion. Once more, note the highly successful use of wooden timbers.

Four weeping ash (above) dominate this grassy enclosure which, in atmosphere, is reminiscent of the shady area so often to be found in the centre of a southern French town. The omission of other plantings underlines an understatement which is one of the major characteristics of this garden.

This handsome door (left), which is in fact leading nowhere, terminates a cross path and succeeds in turning a dead end into a point of interest. An imaginative touch has been to pick out a fleur-de-lis on each of the two panels.

Placed in front of the door is this most intriguing box square (below). The positioning and formation of the plants accurately imitates the placement of the granite sets which surround it.

Everywhere in the garden an eye for detail shows through. Here (above) box hedging is angled to the descent of the steps to give them a neat and definitive edge.

Box spirals like this one (right) require a great deal of time and patience in the making before they achieve the desired effect. Once fully grown twice year clipping, in spring and again in late summer, should keep them in shape.

Looking back towards the entrance to the garden, the way in which the whole is designed to be totally concealed becomes apparent. The gateway lies in fact on the right, approached through the curtains of yew, distinctly separate and removed from the overall plan. The arresting sculpture, one of a number of pieces within the garden, is titled 'Blade' and is by Andrew Griffiths.

## A Garden of Pots

Incredible as it may at first appear, this garden is completely made up of plants grown in pots and containers. Realizing that the area available to them did not permit a garden in the traditional sense, the owners opted to satisfy their love of foliage and flowers by growing them in an ingenious and highly individual manner. The result is a clever and well thought out arrangement which makes extraordinary use of a limited space and yet which meets the needs of the true gardener.

Of course gardening like this is not without its problems. Watering during hot, dry periods must be carried out regularly, often twice daily, and is, on this scale, demanding in terms of both energy and time. To keep plants in top condition a programme of systematic feeding is necessary and always a watchful eye must be cast for pests.

This fine, well established hedge gives all the appearance of having been in place for many, many years. Remarkably it too, along with everything else in the garden, is grown in containers, this time in old tubs.

Room has been found to create this relaxed sitting out area where predominantly foliage plants contribute to an overall restful atmosphere. Tucked into a corner on the left of the entrance this tiny courtyard offers a high degree of seclusion and privacy. Dark green garden furniture is very much in tune with the scheme.

Note the wall mounted container which houses generous swags of ivy.

Few people would give more than passing thought to the idea, let alone possibility, of growing Irish yews in pots. And yet these splendid examples are well and truly contained. That they succeed so well is testimony to the care and attention which their owners give to them and to the garden as a whole. Here they mark the entrance which gives access to the conservatory, the door of which is surrounded with a miniature pot-grown herb garden.

Summer flowering pelargoniums bring the house alive (above) with an abundance of colour during the hottest months of the year. In order to fit in the maximum number of pots, a shelf has been fixed immediately below the eaves which now are disguised in a canopy of foliage and flower.

Both outhouses and garage are framed by the tall growing yew trees (left) which provide a vertical accent within a small area. Even the roof space has been utilized to the full with an imaginative selection of small growing conifers and ivies. An old chimney pot, nestling into the corner, gives scope for yet more planting – *Hedera helix* 'Goldheart'.

A bewildering array of pots and all manner of containers make up the main part of the garden approached to the right of the entrance. This is pot gardening on a grand scale and yet what impresses most of all is the quality and condition of each individual plant. Everything is cared for and well nurtured, the requirements of each subject adhered to with an enviable degree of thoroughness. Well clothed trellis is a backdrop to this imaginative display.

Stout, nicely weathered pots grow beautifully bushy box plants which act within the garden as dividers. These can, if desired, be moved at any time from one place to another.

A charmingly positioned water spout surrounded by lush plantings chosen for their variation in texture and form. By introducing water into the garden the owners have successfully, but unobtrusively, added movement and sound.

# Planting a Small Space

This can be the most difficult part of coping with a small garden but even fairly large plants can be accommodated if you know how they grow and how to control them. Which plants you choose will also determine the style of your garden so it is important to select them carefully.

# Trees for Height and Interest

Of course we should all like to grow trees. Few gardeners anywhere can fail to be impressed by the sight of majestic oaks studding a landscape park, nor of an avenue of ancient beech, nor yet of crack willows masking the course of some undetected stream. And even in a more domestic situation to grow ash or elm, chestnut or alder, poplar or walnut must, realistically, remain a dream for most. But that is not to say that those gardening in a restricted space must forfeit the pleasure altogether of enjoying trees in the garden.

Happily there are many small-scale trees, both deciduous and evergreen, which are eminently suitable for inclusion in all but the most minute of gardens. In incorporating them into the design you are, in effect, contributing a sense of scale as well as giving height in what might otherwise prove to be a flat site and one lacking in interest. In deciding which are for you, consider not only the ultimate height and spread, but shape and form, colour and texture of bark, flowering period, possible fruits and berries, as well as interest of leaf and potential autumn show.

*Acer platanoides* **'Drummondii'** A Norway maple noted for its variegated leaf where a broad margin of white surrounds a fresh green central area. To obtain the true type, a grafted specimen must be had. 6 × 4.5m/20 × 15ft

*Cornus controversa* **'Variegata'** Very, very slow but almost without equal. Horizontal branches in time form a series of tiers, each clothed with creamy-yellow leaves turning to white. An excellent subject to grow as a specimen. 4.5 × 4.5m/15 × 15ft

***Halesia monticola*** Flowering in late spring and early summer, the snowdrop tree is a most elegant addition to the garden. However, for best results this native of North America requires lime-free soil. 4 × 3m/13 × 10ft

***Pyrus salicifolia* 'Pendula'** An ornamental pear of a weeping habit with distinctive, silvery-grey, willow-like leaves. Small white flowers in spring are later followed with tiny, inedible pears. Enjoys a sunny spot. 6 × 4.5m/20 × 15ft

***Robinia pseudoacacia* 'Frisia'** This form of false acacia is noted for its spreading layers of golden yellow foliage which keeps its colour throughout the entire season. Unfussy about soil and situation. 8 × 6m/26 × 20ft

***Caragana arborescens* 'Lorbergii'** Sometimes known as the pea tree on account of late spring, pea-like flowers, this tough plant heralds from the wastes of Siberia making it most suitable for a windy situation. 4 × 4m/13 × 13ft

*Magnolia* × *loebneri* **'Leonard Messel'** So many of the spring-flowering magnolias are a lovely choice for the small garden, particularly where the soil is lime free. In normal soil conditions, add a mulch of well-rotted compost each spring. 8 × 6m/26 × 20ft

*Laburnum watereri 'Vossii'* Well loved for the long yellow tassels which appear in early summer. A light, graceful tree which, casting dappled shade, allows other plants to be grown around it. 4.5 × 3m/15 × 10ft

Startlingly beautiful. The intense blue of an early spring sky highlights the purity of the starry flowered *Magnolia stellata*, which can be grown as a small tree or a shrub (see page 138). An underplanting of the bluish-lilac bulb, *Chionodoxa luciliae* or glory of the snow, would complete the picture.

*Malus* × *schiedeckeri* **'Red Jade'** Of weeping habit, this flowering crab apple produces long-lasting red fruits during the autumn. Many forms of malus are ideally suited to the smaller garden and all blossom well in the spring. 4 × 6m/13 × 20ft

*Prunus* **'Amanogawa'** The attraction of this particular Japanese cherry is its column-like habit making it ideal for a small space. There are, however, a wide range of prunus from which to choose, most of which are easy to grow. Flowers in spring. 6 × 2m/20 × 6ft

*Tamarix tetrandra* Most widely grown in coastal areas as a windbreak, this variety of tamarisk is smothered in pale pink plumes in summer creating a wonderful, feathery effect. Hard prune in late winter or early spring. 4 × 4m/13 × 13ft

*Salix caprea* **'Kilmarnock'** A popular choice where space is limited, the Kilmarnock willow is clothed with silvery catkins in the spring. Best in moisture retentive soil where it will be quick to establish. 2 × 2m/6 × 6ft

Here in 'A Garden Writer's Garden' (see page 62) the Kilmarnock willow has been closely clipped to form a splendid mophead. This unusual treatment results in a tree with added emphasis, well suited to a formal situation.

*Salix alba* subsp. *vitellina* **'Britzensis'** Winter sunshine glows on the pollarded stems of this form of willow. Carried out in the early part of the year such severe pruning keeps this shrubby tree to a manageable size. 3 × 3m/10 × 10ft

Fully clothed by midsummer, this represents a single season's growth making 'Britzensis' a suitable subject with which to screen out an unsightly view or to make an informal boundary.

***Laurus nobilis*** Bay will lend itself readily to shaping when it will make an attractive specimen tree of compact size. Aromatic, evergreen leaves are much in demand to flavour casseroles and stews. E, 12 × 10m/39 × 33ft

***Carpinus betulus*** Common hornbeam may, as here, be kept to a moderate size by clipping to shape. As an alternative it may be grown as a dense hedge when it will keep its leaves over the winter. 12 × 8m/39 × 26ft

***Euonymus fortunei*** Here an evergreen euonymus has been trimmed in such a way as to become a standard tree. Growth is further restricted by keeping it in a tub. 5 × 5m/16 × 16ft

***Acer palmatum* var. *dissectum*** As the year advances so the dark-leafed foliage of this slow growing maple turns to bright red. Plant in a position away from sunlight and any damaging winds. 1.5 × 2.4m/5 × 8ft

***Amelanchier lamarckii*** Young copper-coloured foliage sets off white flowers in spring to be followed by edible summer berries and, finally, spectacular autumnal tints. All of this, and an ability to flourish in most situations. 4.5 × 4.5m/15 × 15ft

***Acer palmatum atropurpureum*** Bronze leaves redden with the approach of autumn making for a fiery display. Many of the smaller acers are most garden worthy plants, all with interesting branch structure. 4.5 × 4.5m/15 × 15ft

***Rhus typhina*** Glorious autumn colour is the outstanding feature of the Stag's Horn Sumach. Grow in any position but watch out for suckers which should be removed as they appear. Crimson fruits are borne in spikes in late summer. 3 × 3m/10 × 10ft

***Sorbus vilmorinii*** The attraction of this graceful tree is twofold: flame foliage in the autumn and decorative pink fruits. As with all the mountain ashes, it will thrive in sun or part shade. 5 × 5m/16 × 16ft

◆ S. *'Joseph Rock' is another good choice. Its yellow berries are, more often than not, disregarded by the birds.*

***Clerodendrum trichotomum*** An outstanding small tree when the starry white flowers in late summer are followed by turquoise berries carried at the centre of a crimson calyx. These appear to drape the tree in lustrous jewels. 4 × 4m/13 × 13ft

***Acer griseum*** The paper-bark maple is most aptly named. Cinnamon-coloured bark which peels, autumn colour and an attractive shape all contribute to the desirability of this small tree. 8 × 6m/26 × 20ft

Small, slow growing conifers add year-round interest, are low on maintenance and are most suitable for areas where space is in short supply. In this garden the focus has been directed towards colour and form.

An Irish yew, *Taxus baccata* 'Fastigiata', plays host to a climbing rose, demonstrating the need in a small garden to maximize all available space. The yew, ultimately, will reach a height of some 4.5m/15ft.

***Abies balsamea* f. *hudsonia*** Forming a rounded, dome-shape, this very small conifer is noted for its bright green, new growth in the springtime. Most appropriate for a rock or alpine garden. E, 1 × 1m/3 × 3ft

***Chamaecyparis lawsoniana* 'Minima Aurea'** Within this scree bed this dwarf conifer gives welcome and much needed height. The foliage, in this the early part of the year, tones with other plantings. E, 1.2 × 1.2m/4 × 4ft

*Juniperus communis* **'Compressa'** For something really tiny, then choose this column-like form of juniper. Grey-green branches are tightly packed ensuring a shapely tree even when fully grown. E, 75 × 15cm/30 × 6in

*Juniperus sabina* **'Tamariscifolia'** The spreading habit of the Savin juniper makes it ideal as ground cover or to spread over a low wall or to clothe a difficult bank. Foliage is an attractive blue-green. E, 1 × 2m/3 × 6ft

*Picea* var. *albertiana* **'Conica'** Bright, fresh foliage tips are a mark of this small spruce of compact shape. A perfect cone, it is ideal either for the rockery or for a container. E, 2 × 1m/6 × 3ft

*Thuja orientalis* **'Aurea Nana'** Oval in shape, the golden yellow branches point upwards. During the winter the foliage turns to an attractive bronzy-green. Perfectly at home in the alpine garden. E, 1m × 75cm/3ft × 30in

# Shrubs — Border Structure

Borders which are entirely made up of annuals and perennials have a tendency to look flat and uninteresting once the main flowering season is past. This is particularly so in late autumn or early spring when old stems have been cut back to ground level and the earth is bare.

By planting mixed borders, where shrubs and herbaceous plants are combined, it is possible to achieve a much more balanced, structured look which will stand up well at all times of the year. Many shrubs will perform twice in one season, giving flower in the spring or summer to be followed, for example, with bright leaf colour or berries later on.

Fortunately there are many highly attractive shrubs which, on account of their slow growth or restricted size, are very well suited to the small garden. Choose them for interesting leaf, sometimes variegated, sometimes evergreen, for flower, for scent, for fruit and for a spectacular autumn show. Larger shrubs, which may be too desirable to omit altogether from the garden, will usually respond well to judicious pruning, which carried out periodically, will keep them well within bounds. Neither should you be afraid of planting something which, in time, will outgrow its position in the garden. Enjoy it for a number of years and then, when it really does start to take over, remove it. You will then have the pleasure of a space to be filled for which you may well find something completely different.

Of course shrubs do not have to be grown in a border. Many are eminently suited to pot cultivation and will thrive under such conditions providing that they are not allowed to dry out, are fed regularly and do not become pot bound. Growing them like this does mean that it is possible to give them exactly the conditions they require, making it possible to grow lime haters in an area of alkaline soil.

*Chaenomeles* **'Pink Lady'** Crimson flowers, in spring, set against glossy green leaves, will later be followed by quince fruits from which delicious jelly may be made. 3 × 3m/10 × 10ft

*Ribes speciosum* Arching stems carry deep red, fuchsia-like flowers in late spring and early summer. This shrub may effectively be trained against a wall. 2 × 2m/6 × 6ft

**Pieris forrestii 'Forest Flame'** Bright scarlet shoots typify new growth on this slow-growing, evergreen shrub. Plant in acid soil in light shade away from strong sunlight.
◗, E, 2 × 4m/6 × 13ft

◆ *Long panicles of creamy-white flowers appear in the mid-spring.* P. formosa *and* P. japonica *are equally good cultivars.*

**Forsythia × intermedia** This easy to grow spring shrub continues to retain its popularity, not least on account of its early sparkling colour.

Once the flowering period is over, hard prune. This will assist in keeping the shrub to shape and should encourage strong new shoots to come from the base.

Cut sprigs whilst still in bud for a vase indoors where they will flower for many weeks. 3 × 2m/10 × 6ft

**Berberis darwinii** Golden flowers of spring are followed in the autumn with purple berries. Trim after flowering to keep in shape. E, 4 × 4m/13 × 13ft

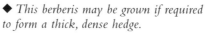

◆ *This berberis may be grown if required to form a thick, dense hedge.*

**Helianthemum 'Golden Queen'** All the rock roses reward with flowers over a considerable period of time. They especially enjoy a sun-baked position. E, 30cm × 1m/1 × 3ft

**Lupinus arboreus** The tree lupin is in flower throughout the early summer. Vigorous in growth, it is quick to establish. Semi-E, 1.5 × 1.5m/5 × 5ft

◆ *Tree lupins are inclined to be fairly short-lived. However, they are easily grown from self-set seed.*

**Philadelphus coronarius** 'Aureus'
Grown especially for its warm yellow
foliage, this form of mock orange is
well suited to the smaller garden.
Avoid planting in full sunlight which
can, on occasion, cause scorching of
new growth.

Partner the yellow leaves with the
deep purple flowers of a clematis such
as *C.* 'Polish Spirit' or 'Burma Star'.
2 × 2m/6 × 6ft

**Azara lanceolata** Very pretty, rather
wispy flowers in spring are set off by
long, tapering shiny green leaves.
E, 2 × 2m/6 × 6ft

◆ *Slightly tender, azara repays for
growing against a wall in a sunny,
sheltered spot.*

**Fothergilla major** A delightful, slow-
growing shrub producing sweetly
scented flowers in the early part of
the year to be followed by vivid
autumn colour. 3 × 3m/10 × 10ft

◆ *Include this shrub within a mixed
border. It will be many years before it
outgrows its space.*

**Potentilla fruticosa** One of many
named forms of dwarf, ground-cover
shrubs which flower almost
continuously throughout the summer.
1.2 × 1.2m/4 × 4ft

**Daphne × burkwoodii** Enjoy deliciously scented daphnes in the first part of the year when their fragrance can fill the entire garden. Slow-growing, they are best afforded some shelter from cold winds. 1.2 × 1.2m/4 × 4ft

◆ *Here the soft pink and white flowers of the daphne are teamed with the violet-blue of Clematis macropetala 'Maidwell Hall'.*

**Buddleja crispa** Possibly one of the loveliest of all buddlejas with grey-green, felted leaves. Not totally hardy, it must be given a warm, protected situation, possibly against a south facing wall. Flowers late summer. ○, 2.4 × 2.4m/8 × 8ft

**Syringa × persica** A compact form of lilac which is beautifully scented and which carries a second crop of flowers in late summer and early autumn. Prune lightly when the first flowers of spring are spent. 2 × 2m/6 × 6ft

***Weigela florida* 'Variegata'** Variegated foliage ensures that this shrub retains interest the whole summer long. The mass of pink bloom appears in the early spring. All weigelas enjoy a sunny, open position in the garden. ○, 1.5 × 1.5m/5 × 5ft

◆ *For late summer cover the weigela with one of the small flowered texensis or viticella clematis. Both of these types are hard pruned in the late winter.*

***Lonicera tatarica*** Delightful pink and white flowers cluster together during late spring and early summer on this unusual, and seldom seen, shrubby honeysuckle. 1.2 × 1.2m/4 × 4ft

***Prunus tenella* 'Firehill'** An ideal shrub to include at the back of a spring border for its lovely, candyfloss pink flowers. *Prunus × cistena* is a white flowered form with deep purple leaves. ○, 2 × 2m/6 × 6ft

*Viburnum plicatum* A splendid, white flowered shrub whose horizontal branches are decked with blooms in the late spring. Pictured in Mirabel Osler's garden (see page 62), regular pruning keeps it to size. 3 × 4m/10 × 13ft

*Magnolia stellata* Star-shaped flowers appear on the bare stems in the early spring. Very slow-growing, plant away from the morning sun which can cause damage to frosted blooms. 3 × 4m/10 × 13ft

*Chaenomeles speciosa* **'Nivalis'** Train this fairly fast growing quince against a wall where it will produce creamy-white flowers continuously in springtime. Cut back side shoots by midsummer. 2.4 × 5m/8 × 16ft

*Exochorda* × *macrantha* **'The Bride'** Amongst the loveliest of shrubs, this form of exochorda is most aptly named. Wreathed in flower for the spring it is ideally suited as a host plant for a late climber. ○, 2.4 × 3m/8 × 10ft

***Viburnum × juddii*** Deeply fragrant spring flowers appear pink in bud, later turning to white. This viburnum succeeds best in soil which is free-draining rather than moisture retentive. 1.5 × 1.5m/5 × 5 ft

***Spiraea nipponica* 'Snowmound'** Early summer sees this easy-to-grow shrub heavily laden with pure white flowers borne upon long, arching stems. Easily kept in shape by clipping once the flowers are over. 2.4 × 2.4m/8 × 8ft

***Choisya* 'Aztec Pearl'** Another form of Mexican orange blossom which is a change from the more widely grown *C. ternata*. As free flowering, it has distinctively shaped long, tapering leaves. E, 2 × 2m/6 × 6ft

***Rhododendron* Hybrid 'Bric-à-Brac'** Flowers bloom as early as the late winter but may be vulnerable to sharp frosts. Evergreen foliage ensures a point of interest at all times. All rhododendrons prefer light shade and neutral to acid soil. E, 1.5 × 1.5m/5 × 5ft

# Roses – Queen of Shrubs

Romantically named, scented with such sweet perfume, coloured in soft, alluring hues, it is little wonder that for many the rose is placed first among all shrubs.

Fortunately there is no reason at all why any garden, however small, should be denied at least one of these choicest of shrubs. From old-fashioned types, steeped in history, to free-flowering climbers, from modern bush roses to those small enough for the tiniest patio, there is something for every situation.

**'Iceberg'** No-one can but admire the habit of this prolific Floribunda with its charming buds opening to wide double blooms. Ideal for a mixed border where it will flower for many months on end. 1.2 × 1.2m/4 × 4ft

◆ *'Iceberg' may be hard pruned during the late winter to produce a compact bush.*

**'Yvonne Rabier'** A dwarf polyantha rose with small, double white flowers which are clustered together. 1.2 × 1m/4 × 3ft

**'Little White Pet'** Small enough to grow in a pot where it will happily produce a succession of dainty flowers. 60 × 60cm/2 × 2ft

**'Gentle Touch'** This truly is a miniature rose for anywhere where space really is restricted. 45cm/1½ft

Growing roses as standards is one way of overcoming a lack of space. In this situation the velvety blooms of the classically shaped 'Royal William' rise over a base of *Hedera canariensis*. The fast-growing, half hardy ivy acts as an ideal foil to the deeply crimson rose flowers. Frequent dead-heading of the rose will ensure repeat flowering.

Standard roses may be used either as a centrepiece to a border to give much needed height, or to provide a miniature avenue on either side of a small path. Whatever, they are most appropriate in formal or semi-formal gardens.

**'Jacques Cartier'** The appeal of this compact, repeat flowering Damask rose lies in the very full flower and the delicious fragrance. 1.2 × 1m/ 4 × 3ft

**'The Fairy'** Lovely sprays of delicate pale-pink rosettes, each one perfumed. Ideally placed at the front of a border to be appreciated fully. 60cm x 1m/2 × 3ft

**'Cécile Brunner'** Affectionately named the sweetheart rose. Sweetly scented, shell-pink blooms are shaped like a miniature Hybrid Tea. Lovely in a massed planting. 1m x 60cm/3 × 2ft

**'Heritage'** One of many recent introductions which as a group have become known as English Roses. They combine repeat flowering with a sturdy, compact habit. The cupped blooms of 'Heritage' are noticeably large and possess a strong fragrance. 1.2 × 1.2m/4 × 4ft

◆ *All of these roses may have their canes pruned by one half or more in winter.*

**'Amber Queen'** Deep yellow-amber blooms are matched with foliage which is subtly tinted bronze. A spreading Floribunda with a sweet scent. 60 × 60cm/2 × 2ft

**'The Pilgrim'** Shiny green leaves set off rosettes of soft yellow on this freely flowering English Rose. 1.1 × 1m/3½ × 3ft

**'Symphony'** Similar in size and habit to 'The Pilgrim', this rose carries plentiful, medium-green leaves over which are numerous scented blooms. 1 × 1m/3 × 3ft

A FURTHER SELECTION OF ROSES

The list of roses suitable for the small garden, on account of their size and habit, is almost without limit. Any one of the following would be deserving of a place and are recommended for their suitability:

'Agnes'
'Alfred de Dalmas'
'De Meaux'
'Fimbriata'
'Hermosa'
'La Ville de Bruxelles'
'Léda'
'Mundi'
'Nathalie Nypels'
'Old Blush China'
R. pimpinellifolia
'Pink Bells'
'Pretty Polly'
'Simba'
'Souvenir de la Malmaison'
'Stanwell Perpetual'

**'Mountbatten'** A useful border rose which with its dark foliage and luminous double flowers would not look amiss in many garden schemes. 1.2 × 1m/4 × 3ft

◆ *All roses will benefit from an annual application of a rose fertilizer.*

# Climbers – Front Line Candidates

That climbers climb, and in so doing occupy very little space at ground level, makes them invaluable plants for the small garden where space is, inevitably, restricted. Not only that, but they provide an almost limitless range of form, habit, flower colour, leaf texture and shape, as well as suggesting something of interest for even the least promising and most difficult of situations.

Use climbers, particularly those which are ever-green, to help block out unsightly surroundings, to screen utilities, to mask unattractive walls and fences or to draw the eye away from a less than appealing viewpoint. Trained to scramble through host plants, such as trees and shrubs, climbers may be used to introduce a secondary canopy of colour and interest at a level above and beyond more traditional plantings on the ground.

Given some support, which may be no more than a simple post, climbers may be used to create much needed height in otherwise flat areas. Many will respond well to pot cultivation and so may be included in even the tiniest of patio gardens. Used with generosity of spirit, and an eye to effect, climbers will reward the gardener with something attractive throughout each month of the year.

*Clematis macropetala* **'Markham's Pink'** Delightful sugar-pink flowers smother this clematis both in the early spring and again, but less freely, in autumn. Pruning is restricted to the removal of any dead or weak shoots. 1.8m/6ft

*Clematis alpina* **'Frances Rivis'** (shown opposite) is also early into flower. Here the semi-double, violet-blue flowers are complemented with attractive, fresh foliage. Pruning is the same as for the macropetala types. 1.8m/6ft

*Clematis alpina* **'Ruby'** Plant this charming spring-flowering clematis in a sunny spot to capture the intensity of the dusky mauve-red flowers. Consider combining two, or more, clematis of similar habit for a really well furnished look. 1.8m/6ft

◆ *Alpina clematis produce prominent fluffy seed-heads. Visually these are an additional bonus and remain until well into winter. Plants raised from seed will not, sadly, exactly reproduce the parent.*

*Clematis alpina* **'Willy'** Pale pink sepals, which nicely taper to a point, are highlighted with a touch of cyclamen pink. All of these spring clematis of moderate growth would be suitable for a pot or container. 1.8m/6ft

*Clematis macropetala* **'Maidwell Hall'** All of the macropetala clematis are absolute treasures and may always be relied upon to put on one of the best displays of spring. Preferring some shade, they will still perform well in sun. 1.8m/6ft

*Clematis montana* **'Elizabeth'** Lovely in flower in spring but, as these thick stems show, not entirely suitable for the small garden. Use to smother a shed or to climb into a perimeter tree. 6m/20ft

*Clematis chrysocoma* Not dissimilar to the montanas but considerably less vigorous. The soft pink of the spring flowers is set off by distinctly bronzed foliage. After flowering lightly prune to check growth. 6m/20ft

*Clematis* **'Nelly Moser'** Probably one of the most popular, and certainly one of the best known, of the large-flowered hybrids. Position in partial shade to prevent the rosy-mauve sepals from fading in strong sunlight. Spring flowers are repeated in late summer. 3m/10ft

◆ *Shown here growing through* Ceanothus *'Puget Blue', 'Nelly Moser' illustrates one of countless ways in which clematis may be teamed with shrubs to produce colourful and eye-catching partnerships.*

*Clematis* **'Lady Northcliffe'** Seldom without flower from mid to late summer thus worthy of inclusion in any garden. 1.8m/6ft

*Clematis* **'Étoile de Malicorne'** This most striking of clematis is used here to clothe the lower reaches of a yew hedge. Flowers early summer. 1.8m/6ft

◆ *Clematis do not have to be grown vertically. They are equally happy when trained to cover the ground.*

*Clematis* **'Mrs. Cholmondeley'** Vigorous growth of this lovely hybrid may be restricted by hard pruning in the early part of the year. Where this is carried out, 'Mrs. Cholmondeley' becomes suitable for growing in a pot. Flowers from early summer. 6m/20ft

◆ *This pale lavender-blue is an easy colour to associate with others. Here it is planted to climb through a rose.*

**Clematis 'Kathleen Wheeler'** The white of this rose is a perfect backdrop to the plummy-mauve flowers of this bushy climber. 2.4m/8ft

◆ *'Kathleen Wheeler' should provide a respectable second flowering in the autumn.*

**Clematis 'Elsa Späth'** A mass of midsummer flowers is followed by a second flush later in the year. Unfussy and easy to grow. 1.8m/6ft

**Clematis 'Barbara Dibley'** The moderate growth of this gorgeous purple-red hybrid makes it most appropriate for any number of situations. Grow it in a pot, up a pole, against a trellis or into a low shrub. Flowers early summer. 1.8m/6ft

◆ *For deepest colour grow away from very strong sunlight which can cause noticeable fading.*

***Clematis* 'Niobe'** To achieve the maximum number of these rich ruby-red flowers over the longest possible time, prune, 'Niobe' only lightly at the start of the year. A hard prune will delay the flowering period until late summer. 2.4m/8ft

◆ *'Niobe' is an excellent subject to grow into a small, early flowering tree or shrub. It would be particularly at home trained through the early magnolias.*

Pictured right are three highly desirable clematis to provide colour from midsummer onwards.

First to flower is *C.* × *jackmanii*, well known to gardeners and non-gardeners alike. A strong colour, good performance and reliability combine to make it a popular choice.

Late-flowering viticella hybrids are amongst the most appealing of all clematis. Blooming for up to three months they require little beyond an annual hard prune, at which time they benefit from a dressing of good garden compost. Shown here are 'Madame Julia Correvon', in shades of deep red, and 'Purpurea Plena Elegans' whose double rosy-purple flowers are an absolute delight.

Try growing 'Purpurea Plena Elegans' through the shrub *Callicarpa bodinieri* var. *geraldii*. In late summer the foliage turns purplish and each branch is decked with small, lustrous berries, the exact tone of the clematis.

***Wisteria floribunda*** It is not, as might be thought, essential to train a wisteria against a wall. This one has been very successfully grown up a stout pole, an idea which could be copied in a comparatively small space. Flowers early summer. ○, 9m/30ft

***Wisteria floribunda* 'Alba'** Racemes of pure white flowers in early summer. Combine with fresh foliage to clothe the walls of this house, thus helping to disguise brickwork. Wisteria may be kept within bounds by pruning in winter and summer. ○, 9m/30ft

***Lonicera etrusca*** Unfortunately this beautiful creamy-yellow honeysuckle is not reliably hardy. However, it is well worth trying in a sheltered, sunny spot or even to be grown against a support in a large container. Flowers summer/autumn. ○, 4m/13ft

***Lonicera japonica* 'Halliana'** A rapidly growing evergreen whch could be used to screen out a more utilitarian part of the garden. Flowers, which appear in summer, are perfumed. E, 4m/13ft

**Hydrangea anomala petiolaris** Slow to establish, the self-clinging, climbing hydrangea is a splendid climber with which to cover a dull wall, producing these large, creamy-white flowers in summer even in a shady position. 8m/26ft

◆ *When planting climbers, try not to think singly. The hydrangea could easily host a late-flowering clematis as well as, possibly, an annual pea.*

**Actinidia kolomikta** Such unusual leaf markings, almost as if they had been splashed with paint, distinguish this climber of moderate growth. Plant in full sun to achieve best variegation. 3.5m/12ft

◆ *Do not worry about climbers exceeding the spaces intended for them. Judicious pruning from time to time will cause no harm whatsoever and will help to keep things manageable.*

# Climbing Roses

Roses epitomize early summer with their heavenly fragrance and lovely, lovely blooms in a range of delicious colours. In the small garden it may not always be possible to cultivate some of the old-fashioned shrub roses on account of the space they demand if they are to be grown well. An easy solution is to include in the garden a number of climbing roses which will, whilst occupying a minimum amount of soil space, convey a sense of rich plenty and tradition.

Make your choice with care. Rambler roses are likely to prove far too vigorous and even some of the climbers may, when established, be in danger of outgrowing their allotted space. Select, where possible, those with a recurrent flowering pattern for they will provide interest over a much longer period.

Pruning of climbing roses consists of removing dead or diseased wood in early spring. Cut back side shoots that have previously flowered to about 7.5cm/3in long. Tie in strong new shoots as they develop.

Climbing roses have stiff stems which are not easy to tie back to their support once they have become woody, so it is sensible to check them regularly in a confined space.

*Rosa* **'Blush Noisette'** An excellent choice for an archway, against a wall or trellis or to cover a pergola. These pretty pinky-white flowers, sweetly scented, will be continuous all summer long. 2.2m/7ft

*Rosa* **'Golden Showers'** An advantage of this free-flowering, fragrant climber is that it will provide a succession of blooms even when grown against a sunless wall. 3m/10ft

*Rosa* **'Climbing Iceberg'** The climbing form of this popular Floribunda produces large trusses of pure white flowers unstintingly over a long period. Foliage remains fresh and glossy. 3m/10ft

*Rosa* **'Variegata di Bologna'** Handsome, cupped flowers of creamy-white which are distinctly marked with crimson-purple stripes. This rose is only slightly recurrent but its unusual colourings make up for that. 3m/10ft

*Rosa* **'Buff Beauty'** This wonderfully scented, warm apricot flowered hybrid musk rose may easily be trained as a climber. Double flowers continue to bloom over several weeks. 3m/10ft

# *Wall Shrubs*

In a small garden, where every plant must more than earn its keep, learn to experiment. It is often the case that many of the very desirable and highly prized shrubs available in garden centres and from specialist nurseries are slightly on the tender side and deemed not to be fully hardy.

Always remember that in an enclosed space, often sheltered from cold winds and the worst of frosts, you are possibly creating a warm micro-climate where many plants, previously thought of as unsuitable for the garden, will not only survive but thrive.

Close planting will also afford protection from the worst of the weather and you may always, in periods of intense cold, place bracken, sacking or any other porous material around the base of the shrub.

**Abutilon megapotamicum** Placed against a sunny wall this shrub will reward with an abundance of these brightly coloured, red and yellow flowers towards summer's end. Arching stems will need to be supported and tied-in. E, 2.4m/8ft

◆ *Before planting a wall shrub take time to secure support wires firmly in place. These will make subsequent tying-in much easier.*

**Carpenteria californica** Evergreen foliage of a glossy, bright green forms a background to these stunning, fragrant flowers which bloom throughout the mid-summer. A lovely shrub deserving of a place in every sheltered garden. 1.5 × 1.5m/5 × 5ft

◆ *As with many shrubs, if caught by extreme cold, carpenteria will regenerate from old wood, even renewing itself from the base.*

**Rhodochiton atrosanguineus** Heralding from Mexico this exotic climber may, in cold areas, be grown as an annual. After the red and purple flowers throughout the summer balloon-like seed capsules appear. ○, 3m/10ft

**Robinia kelseyi** Brittle branches which break easily make the training of this most attractive shrub something of a problem. However, its flowers in late spring are an extremely impressive sight. ○, 2.4m/8ft

**Passiflora caerulea** Wherever it is grown the passion flower always excites interest. The extraordinary exquisite blooms in summer and autumn are followed by small, orange fruits. ○, 6m/20ft

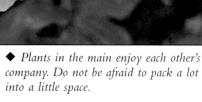

**Lavatera maritima bicolor** A free-flowering tree mallow which should be pruned hard in the early spring. Propagation is by means of easily rooted cuttings. 1.5m/5ft

◆ *Plants in the main enjoy each other's company. Do not be afraid to pack a lot into a little space.*

**Eccremocarpus scaber** Orange and red tubular flowers in summer give the Chilean glory vine a vibrancy which may be used to inject life into dull areas. ○, 4m/13ft

**Ceanothus 'Blue Mound'** A glorious, blue-flowered shrub for the early summer which, lovely as it is, would make a superb host for any number of contrasting or complementary climbers. A clematis to flower with the ceanothus could be followed by another for midsummer and even one for later on. ○, E, 1.5 × 2m/5 × 6ft

**Abutilon × suntense** As an insurance against loss during bouts of very cold weather, take cuttings of this fast-growing shrub. Flowers in late spring and early summer. ○, 2.4m/8ft

**× Fatshedera lizei** Arranged against a wall these grand leaves would make a splendid backdrop to virtually any planting. Prefers moist soil. E, 2 × 3m/6 × 10ft

**Solanum crispum 'Glasnevin'** Smothered in flower for most of the summer, this remarkable shrub, nearly always wall-trained, is breathtakingly wonderful. Frost hardy to −5°C/23°F. ○, E or semi-E, 6m/20ft

◆ *Regular pruning, best carried out in spring, will keep solanum to the required size.*

**Callistemon pallidus** Flowers of the 'bottle brush' in early summer are a delight not only for their appearance but also for the way in which they cry out to be touched. Evergreen foliage is lemon-scented. To achieve success with callistemon soil should be acidic, well drained and the plant placed in full sun. E, 3m/10ft

# Perennials – Flowers For Every Season

Time was when every garden, almost without exception, boasted an herbaceous border. Principally consisting of summer flowering perennials, these studies in horticulture reached their peak in mid-season, to be sustained in some instances, usually with the addition of Michaelmas daisies, well into autumn. Exacting in every respect, and totally labour intensive, such borders have by and large in recent times been replaced by those which are mixed, made up of trees, shrubs, bulbs, annuals and, of course, perennials.

Gardening on whatever scale, perennials are as invaluable as they are essential. Not only do they cover an enormous range of flowering plants, but they also include fashionable grasses, sedges and ferns. Not all, it must be said, are suitable for the small garden. Some, on account of their height and spread, a tendency to be invasive or to seed around too freely, must be omitted. Others with a very short flowering season, or a reluctance to flower, however desirable, should be passed over in favour of those which represent much better value. And for this there is no shortage of choice.

However, do not allow yourself to be too cautious. A garden filled with perennial plants of uniform height and even spread will be totally lacking in interest. Some plants may be included simply on account of their size where their greatest impact will be made in a restricted space. Likewise tall-growing plants placed at the front of the border will introduce variety of pattern and help to avoid any suggestion of monotony.

*Epimedium* × *youngianum* '**Roseum**' Delightful rose-coloured flowers rise from a base of prettily shaped leaves in the early spring. Plant in a shady position and cut back to ground level in the late winter just before new growth commences. 25 × 30cm/10in × 1ft

*Primula vulgaris* A cool, slightly shady spot is an ideal place in which to grow clumps of the early-flowering primrose. They are particularly effective in association with wood anemones and tiny, wild daffodils. 10cm/4in

***Convallaria majalis*** Unfussy about where it is grown, often thriving in total shade, deliciously scented lily-of-the-valley should be placed somewhere where it may slowly increase over the years. Flowers open in spring. ◐, ●, 20cm/8in

***Lamium maculatum* 'White Nancy'** Lighten a dull corner with this free-flowering, variegated form of dead-nettle. Whilst it will spread, it is easily removed if and when it exceeds its allocated space. 15 × 60cm/6in × 2ft

***Dicentra* 'Bacchanal'** An unusual but very fine form of the bleeding heart. Deepest red flowers are borne in profusion over finely cut, grey-green leaves throughout the spring. 30 × 30cm/1in × 1ft

***Primula denticulata* var. *alba*** White rounded heads of this drumstick primula make a wonderful show at the beginning of the year. Most primulas appear to enjoy a cool position in moisture-retentive soil. ◐, 20 × 30cm/8in × 1ft

***Uvularia grandiflora*** Grow the bellwort for its graceful and certainly different spring flowers. Ideally it prefers a moist, slightly acid soil in some shade but should prosper under normal garden conditions. ◯, 30 × 30cm/1 × 1ft

***Ajuga reptans* 'Catlin's Giant'** In spring large blue flower heads appear to soar above metallic, purple leaves on this particularly good form of bugle. Give it sufficient space to carpet an area of ground, suppressing weeds as it goes. E, 15 × 60cm/6in × 2ft

***Galium ordoratum*** Sweet woodruff is a charming little carpeting plant to grow in a lightly shaded, informal part of the garden. The white star flowers appear in spring and are long-lasting. 20 × 30cm/8in × 1ft

***Iris graminea*** Shaded purple flowers in late spring nestle amongst lustrous foliage in the plum tart iris. Its common name derives from the scent of the flowers, smelling exactly of cooked plums. For partial shade. ◑, 30 × 30cm/ 1 × 1ft

***Sedum* 'Ruby Glow'** For end–of–year colour when the crimson flowers, much loved by butterflies, come into their own. A more compact form of the widely grown *S.* 'Autumn Joy'. ○, 30 × 30cm/1 × 1ft

***Campanula punctata* 'Rubriflora'** Light maroon tubular bells provide summer colour over many weeks. Here companion plantings are hardy geraniums and diascias, each plant encouraged to intermingle with its neighbour. 30 × 30cm/1 × 1ft

◆ *Close planting of this kind ensures that very few weeds have the space or light in which to germinate. Furthermore, it gives a border a well-furnished appearance.*

*Phlox carolina* **'Bill Baker'** Constant dead-heading will reward with a succession of flowers from early summer, the main flowering period, through very many weeks. This is a plant for either sun or partial shade. 30 × 30cm/1 × 1ft

*Phlox divaricata* **'May Breeze'** An early-flowering phlox in cool shades of white with a subtle hint of lilac. Placed at the front of the border, its delicious scent is immediately apparent. 30 × 20cm/1ft × 8in

*Dianthus gratianopolitanus* All of the old-fashioned pinks, and this one is no exception, like to be baked in full sun. They will tolerate dry, free-draining soil and are easily propagated from cuttings. Summer-flowering. ○, E, 20 × 45cm/8in × 1¹/₂ft

***Geranium renardii*** An attractive, purple-veined flower in early summer is complemented by wonderfully shaped, textured, soft grey-green foliage. This hardy geranium forms a compact clump and makes a very desirable perennial. Cut back in autumn or spring. ◯, 30 × 30cm/ 1 × 1ft

***Geranium endressii*** Most useful as ground cover, growing well in quite difficult situations. A tendency to spread is very easily curtailed. Pretty pink flowers are carried over several weeks in summer. 60 × 60cm/2 × 2ft

***Geranium pratense* 'Mrs. Kendall Clark'** In summer the appeal of this particular cranesbill is the flower colour of very pale, veined, blush lilac. An excellent plant to use as a foil to something much stronger, more bold. 75 × 45cm/ 2½ × 1½ft

***Geranium cinereum* 'Ballerina'** An enchanting, low-growing hardy geranium which never fails to delight. Flowers are carried over a long period in summer and the prettily shaped leaves remain attractive all season. 20 × 30cm/8in × 1ft

*Helleborus orientalis* Early-flowering hellebores are amongst the most desirable of all spring flowers in shades ranging from pure white and yellow, to pale pink, from deepest red to near black. Remove old leaves as buds begin to form. ◐, 45 × 45cm/1¹/₂ × 1¹/₂ft

*Eryngium variifolium* Sea-hollies add texture and form to the border with their distinctive flower heads in late summer which are both rounded and spiky. This one makes a very compact plant. All are completely hardy. O, 45 × 25cm/1¹/₂ft × 10in

*Persicaria campanulata* At the back of the border this hardy perennial will provide colour right up until the first frosts of autumn. Take note of its spreading habit and dig out unwanted growth. 1 × 1m/3 × 3ft

*Euphorbia nicaeensis* An absolutely spectacular plant on account of its wonderful silver foliage. Draw attention to it as a spot plant, or team it with deep purple and darkest plum. O, E, 40 × 60cm/1¹/₂ × 2ft

Using plants together effectively is so very important in a small garden where every picture counts. Here grey-leafed hostas are captured at flowering time alongside the feathery plumes of white and coral astilbes.

◆ *All of the plants illustrated on these pages may be relied upon to give relatively trouble-free, long-term value in terms of foliage and flower.*

*Nepeta* **'Six Hills Giant'** Use all the catmints to provide a soft accent in the border. Once the main summer flowering period is over, cut back to be rewarded with a second flush. ○, 60 × 60cm/2 × 2ft

*Polemonium reptans* **'Lambrook Mauve'** This Jacob's Ladder delights with flowers of washed-out blue-mauve in summer. Lovely to include in a scheme dominated by pale pastel colours or to contrast with old roses. 60 × 60cm/ 2 × 2ft

***Scabiosa caucasica*** Lovely violet-blue scabious are partnered in this setting with the large, flat heads of yarrow, *Achillea filipendula* 'Gold Plate', for an eye-catching summer display. ◯, 60 × 60cm/2 × 2ft

***Salvia sclarea* var. *turkestanica*** A short-lived perennial which is probably best regarded as a biennial. Self-seeded plantlets, easily recognizable, will appear around the parent plant in the spring and flower the following summer. 75 × 30cm/2$^{1}/_{2}$ × 1ft

***Iris pallida* ssp. *pallida*** Bold plantings of irises for early summer give to any border a sense of purpose and of deliberate planning. The effect of one variety is so much better than that of mixed colours. ◯, 45 × 30cm/1$^{1}/_{2}$ × 1ft

◆ *Note how the same tone of the irises is repeated in* Clematis *'The President' which has been used to clothe the wall in the background.*

***Knautia macedonica*** Wine-red, scabious-like knautia is charmingly and informally teamed in a summer display with contrasting spires of lavender-blue veronica. Knautia will readily increase from self-sown seedlings which will be found round and about. 45 × 45cm/$1^{1}/_{2}$ × $1^{1}/_{2}$ft

***Salvia* × *superba* 'Mainacht'** Stiff spikes of deep violet-blue flowers from mid to late summer typify this hardy, border sage. Most noticeable when planted in a drift as in this garden situation. 45 × 45cm/$1^{1}/_{2}$ × $1^{1}/_{2}$ft

***Aquilegia* hybrid** Long-spurred columbines, taking up very little space indeed, should be allowed to self-seed through mixed borders to give a well-furnished look in spring and summer. Where they cross, interesting seedlings will result. 1m × 45cm/3 × $1^{1}/_{2}$ft

***Thalictrum aquilegiifolium*** Use fluffy meadow rue towards the back of the border where it will contribute an air of lightness in summer. Once the flowers are finished, cut off and continue to enjoy pretty foliage. 75 × 60cm/2¹⁄₂ × 2ft

***Paeonia lactiflora* 'Bowl of Beauty'** Amongst the aristocrats of garden plants, peonies should be enjoyed in summer for their wonderful, if somewhat blowzy, flowers and their appealing leaves, often darkly and richly coloured. 1 × 1m/3 × 3ft

***Papaver orientale*** Named varieties of the oriental poppy, often in spectacular shades, are well worth seeking out. Flowering in early summer, their dying foliage needs to be disguised with later plantings. 1m × 60cm/3 × 2ft

***Diascia vigilis*** All of the diascias contribute vibrant colour over a very long period in smmer. Not all are totally hardy so should be afforded some protection during prolonged periods of cold. 45 × 45cm/1¹⁄₂ × 1¹⁄₂ft

*Alstroemeria* **'Ligtu Hybrids'** There is something slightly exotic about the summer blooms of the alstroemeria. In fact this variety is quite hardy given a sunny situation and really good drainage. ○, 60 × 30cm/2 × 1ft

*Lychnis chalcedonica* Long-lasting, scarlet flower heads are used to add a touch of vibrant colour to the early summer border. Consider too the double form as well as pink and white. 1m × 45cm/3 × 1¹/₂ft

*Penstemon* **'Apple Blossom'** All of the penstemons make excellent border plants not least because of their long flowering period in summer. Hardier than is generally thought, delay cutting back until mid-spring. ○, 60 × 45cm/2 × 1¹/₂ft

*Crocosmia* **'Vulcan'** Not dissimilar to *C.* 'Lucifer' but slightly later to flower. Crocosmias are useful plants to sustain interest and colour in the border from mid-summer onwards. 1m × 30cm/3 × 1ft

**Smilacina racemosa** Useful for planting under and around trees where it will produce these flowery plumes in quite shady conditions in late spring. Best results are obtained where the soil is slightly acidic. 75 × 75cm/2¹/₂ × 2¹/₂ft

**Polygonatum × hybridum** Solomon's seal is lovely grown on a bank when the full effect of its arching stems and late spring bell-shaped flowers may be appreciated. Cutworm caterpillars are apt to ravage the foliage later on. 1m × 45cm/3 × 1¹/₂ft

**Sisyrinchium striatum** In summer from iris-like foliage arise rather strange little creamy flowers arranged on stiff spikes. A fairly short-lived plant, it will seed around freely but is seldom a nuisance. A variegated from, *S. striatum* 'Aunt May', is worth growing. 60 × 30cm/2 × 1ft

**Lysimachia clethroides** Somewhat ethereal in appearance, include this perennial where understatement is the order of the day. Charming with other whites, or partnered with blue or the palest of lemon. Flowers in late summer. 1m × 30cm/3 × 1ft

**Dictamnus albus purpureus** A gentle, misty, early summer combination of the pale purple dictamnus set against the snow-white blooms of *Rosa* 'Iceberg'. Slow to establish, it is worth waiting for this perennial to clump up.
60 × 60cm/2 × 2ft

◆ *In a small garden time spent on arranging pleasing and often different colour groupings is never wasted. Therein lies much of the success of the garden.*

**Gillenia trifoliata** There is something rather special about this wonderfully graceful, unassuming hardy perennial which, unaccountably, is seldom seen growing. Use it in summer as a graceful filler between other showier plants.
1m × 60cm/3 × 2ft

**Stachys macrantha** Distinctive, purplish summer flowers are highlighted here with a scattering of the annual white nigella. Place fairly close to the front of the border and look out for a few seedlings. 45 × 45cm/1$^{1}/_{2}$ × 1$^{1}/_{2}$ft

***Kniphofia* 'Little Maid'** Red hot pokers need not be the startling flame colours with which they are so often associated. Here the creamy-yellow spikes, touched with green, are subdued enough for a quiet summer scheme. 60 × 45cm/2 × 1½ft

***Asphodeline lutea*** A rather strange looking perennial made up of a series of yellow, star-like summer flowers hugging a tall-growing, thin-leafed stem. A plant to grow amongst others, rather than alone. 1m × 60cm/3 × 2ft

***Veronica gentianoides* 'Tissington White'** Edge a border, as here, with a row of this pale blue–white veronica. Ground-hugging leaves remain evergreen, the flowers appearing from mid-spring. ○, 25 × 20cm/10 × 8in

◆ *Strong plantings give purpose and meaning to a garden. Too many different plants will, in a small space, rapidly look confusing.*

***Anthemis tinctoria* 'Alba'** It is worth taking the time and trouble regularly to dead-head this perenial to enjoy a succession in mid-summer of these pale, creamy flowers. Cutting back is possibly best delayed until the spring. ◯, 75 × 75cm/2¹/₂ × 2¹/₂ft

***Inula barbata*** These bright yellow daisy flowers may be enjoyed well into the autumn. Place this plant in a position at the front of the border where it will catch most of the sun. ◯, 60 × 45cm/2 × 1¹/₂ft

***Rudbeckia fulgida* 'Goldsturm'** A bold stand of this prolific late summer perennial which, in fact, may be relied upon to flower for several months. In this border it is partnered with *Helenium* 'Golden Youth' of similar colour. ◯, 75 × 45cm/2¹/₂ × 1¹/₂ft

◆ *Do not be in too much of a hurry to cut back in the autumn. Stems, such as these, take on a new life when frosted in winter.*

*Aster × frikartii* **'Mönch'** One of the best of all the Michaelmas daisies because of its long-flowering period from mid-simmer onwards. Here it forms a background to the perennial *Agastache* 'Blue Fortune'. ○, 75 × 45cm/ 2¹/₂ × 1¹/₂ft

◆ *Experiment with placing together different plants but those which share the same colour tones. Clematis 'Mrs. Cholmondeley', not pictured, is of a similar hue to the aster and agastache.*

*Hemerocallis* **'Summer Wine'** A spectacular day lily of a rich wine-red. Swept-back flower heads from mid to late summer possess a velvety quality. Hemerocallis are easy in cultivation and unfussy as to situation. Divide periodically. 1 × 1m/3 × 3ft

*Phlox* **'Norah Leigh'** The attraction of this summer-flowering phlox is not simply its pale pinky-lilac flower but rather its leaves which are variegated cream and green. It enjoys a position in full sun. ○, 75 × 60cm/2¹/₂ × 2ft

As the days of summer lengthen and the approach of autumn gathers pace, so the cone flowers, marked by their stiff daisy heads, come into their own. Pictured here are *Echinacea purpurea* and *E. purpurea* 'White Swan', the latter having a centre which is distinctly green in colour. Both are fully hardy and will tolerate most growing conditions apart from full shade.
75 × 45cm/2½ × 1½ft

***Campanula lactiflora*** Drift this campanula through the back of the summer border or grow it into the lower branches of pastel-flowered shrub roses. A mass of this lovely, soft colour is almost without equal. 1.2m × 60cm/ 4 × 2ft

***Aconitum carmichaelii* 'Barker's Variety'** An intense blue such as this is rarely seen. Late-flowering monkshood, or wolf's bane, is a poisonous plant which somehow in appearance is slightly sinister. 1.5m × 30cm/5 × 1ft

***Campanula latifolia alba*** White flowers give to the border a certain luminosity, and this splendid bellflower is no exception. Plant in slight shade for the greatest intensity of colour. Basal leaves remain evergreen. Summer-flowering. 1.2m × 30cm/4 × 1ft

***Phlox paniculata* 'Fujiyama'** Large flower heads in late summer of pure white are scented. Planted towards the back of the border 'Fujiyama' will add both grace and distinction. ○, 1m × 75cm/3 × 2¹/₂ft

***Crambe cordifolia*** Such a plant as this, with its wonderful, frothy summer flowers, themselves scented, is, at a glance, irresistible. Why not include something as splendid to make a statement whilst adding to the garden a further dimension? ○, 2 × 1.2m/6 × 4ft

◆ *If this is really not for you, then consider the lower-growing gypsophila as a substitute plant. It too gives a very alluring, misty effect.*

***Alcea rugosa*** Tall-growing, perennial hollyhocks, like this one of pale yellow, give height and stature to a garden in summer and early autumn. They are an expression of confidence which is all too easily overlooked.
2m × 45cm/6 × 1¹/₂ft

***Cephalaria gigantea*** For some reason this tall, scabious-like lemon flower remains a stranger to many gardeners. Thin stems, which are easily seen through, enable it to be positioned quite close to the front of the summer border.
2m × 45cm/6 × 1¹/₂ft

***Verbascum chaixii* 'Album'** Stately verbascums, reaching skywards as miniature rockets, are perennials which simply have to be included in the garden. This one is but one of many named varieties. Summer-flowering. 1.5m × 45cm/ 5 × 1¹/₂ft

***Lobelia syphilitica*** Unfortunately this particular lobelia is unlikely to prove hardy in any but the warmest and most sheltered of gardens. However, it should be easy to propagate from cuttings or, indeed, to overwinter in a frost-free glasshouse. Flowers late summer to autumn. 1.2m × 30cm/4 × 1ft

**Delphinium** In some ways no garden should be without such a traditional and much loved summer flower as the delphinium. Select from a wide range of large flowered hybrids available in the most exciting of colours. ○, 2.4 × 1m/8 × 3ft but depends on type.

◆ *As with all tall-growing perennials it is advisable to give some form of support to prevent the collapse of flower spikes in wet and windy conditions.*

**Aster novi–belgii 'Goliath'** Free-flowering asters contribute warmth and colour to late summer borders and help to extend the season of interest well into autumn. Divide on a regular basis in spring. ○, 1.2m × 45cm/ 4 × 1¹/₂ft

**Anemone × hybrida** Japanese anemones are one of the principal delights of the end-of-year garden although with an extended flowering period they belong as much to summer as to autumn. 1.5m × 45cm/5 × 1¹/₂ft

# Annuals, Biennials, Half-Hardy Perennials – for Fast Effects

For continuous colour through much of the growing season, then there is little to rival a show of annuals. Usually raised from seed, these plants will reach flowering point within a very short space of time, to reward thereafter with a succession of blooms freely displayed until the first of the frosts. Little wonder that they remain such a popular choice for pots and containers, for hanging baskets as well as to plug gaps in borders left as spring flowers die away. Extend both interest and the range of colour with biennials, those plants which will flower from seed in their second year, and half-hardy perennials which, in colder areas, are unlikely to survive the worst of winters.

And there is something to satisfy every possible taste, every conceivable garden situation. For sheer brilliance there are the bedding salvias, *Salvia splendens*, French and African marigolds, colourful petunias, blue and purple lobelias and cheerful impatiens. For scent, include old-fashioned stocks, surfinia, nemesia and, of course, fragrant nicotiana, the tobacco plant, with its powerful, heady perfume. To create an exotic look, suggestive of hot, sunny climates, there are lotus plants, half-hardy osteospermums, tender argyranthemums and fabulous gazanias. For those looking for the understated, ethereal look, then try early white nigella to be followed with late flowering, white cosmos.

**Helianthus** Sunflowers are such fun. Allow them to soar up at the back of the border where they will give endless delight to children, and to adults too! ○, 2.2m/7ft or more

**Helichrysum** In addition to the enjoyment of growing these colourful strawflowers in the garden throughout the summer, they may also be very effectively dried for indoor flower arrangements out of season. ○, 60 × 30cm/2 × 1ft

***Clarkia elegans*** Clarkia firmly belongs in the cottage garden tradition where drifts of pink, scarlet and mauve will create an harmonious display in the early summer. ○, 60 × 30cm/2 × 1ft

***Digitalis purpurea*** Traditional, biennial foxgloves remain a firm favourite for mid-summer. Allow them to self-seed in a partially shaded area towards the back of the border. Unwanted seedlings are easily weeded out.
◐, 1.2m × 30cm/4 × 1ft

***Argyranthemum* 'Vancouver'** Tender Paris daisies or marguerites in pink, as here, white or yellow will be in flower for weeks on end. For this reason they are an excellent choice for pots or to fill gaps in summer borders. ○, 1 × 1m/3 × 3ft

***Cosmos*** Annual cosmos may be relied upon for its length of flowering. Easily raised from seed, it is a useful plant with which to extend the period of colour in the border. 1m × 60cm/3 × 2ft

***Arctotis* × *hybrida* 'Wine'** Hot colours, such as this one, are to be found in plenty in these South African daisies. Strictly perennial, they should be treated as an annual in colder areas. Flowers from summer into autumn. ○, 45 × 30cm/1¹/₂ × 1ft

***Felicia amelloides*** Flowers are not at all dissimilar to those of a Michaelmas daisy. However, these clear blue, yellow-centred heads will sparkle with colour all summer long. ○, 45 × 30cm/1¹/₂ × 1ft

***Lavatera trimestris*** A free-flowering, half-hardy annual closely related to the shrubby mallow. Ruby-cerise pink flowers produce an on-going show for months on end. ○, 60 × 30cm/2 × 1ft

**Zonal Pelargonium** Countless varieties ensure the continued popularity of what are widely known as summer geraniums. Stock plants, from which cuttings may be taken, should be kept frost-free. ○, 45cm/1¹/₂ft

No garden can really be complete without a share, however small, of the quintessential sweet William, or *Dianthus barbatus*. A reliable biennial, they may, once established, be left to themselves to set seed and come again. Lovely in the summer border, they also make excellent flowers to cut and arrange in water indoors.

Grow them initially from seed either mixed, in single colours or as named varieties like the salmon 'Newport Pink' or aptly named 'Scarlet Beauty'.

***Nicotiana*** Enticingly perfumed tobacco plants of pale salmon-pink are teamed here with toning impatiens in shades of coral. Such a profusion of blooms is best achieved where the plants are in full sun. ○, 30–90 × 30–45cm/ 1–3 × 1–1¹/₂ft

***Zinnia*** Sown in situ in late spring, zinnias provide a wealth of easy summer colour with an abundance of flowers on long stems making them ideal for cutting. ○, 75 × 30cm/ 2¹/₂ × 1ft

***Nigella damascena*** With such an evocative name as 'love-in-a-mist', it is difficult to resist these easily cultivated, popular annuals principally in shades of blue, but also to be found in rose, pink and white. 45 × 20cm/1¹/₂ft × 8in

**Heliotrope** Deep blue or violet flowers are strongly scented of cherry pie. The leaves, over which rise the corymbs of flowers, are deeply veined and purposeful in appearance. ○, 45 × 30cm/1¹/₂ × 1ft

**Antirrhinum** Snapdragons conjure up memories of childhood, possibly because they are always at home in those small garden plots belonging to young children. These, of intense orange-red, are a small sample of all the bright colours which may be grown. ○, 30 × 15cm/ 1ft × 6in

◆ *Try raising antirrhinums in pots indoors over winter for use as spring-flowering houseplants. Choose F1 hybrids for best blooms.*

**Tagetes patula** French marigolds, in shades of yellow, orange and bronze, produce flowers continuously throughout the summer. Bushy plants, easily raised, account for their widespread popularity and use. ○, 25cm/10in

**Tagetes** This particular variety of French marigold boasts double flowers of rich golden-yellow with markings of mahogany-red. Many named varieties are to be found on the lists of seed merchants. ○, 25cm/10in

**Universal Pansies** Wonderful, cheery faces in all manner of colour combinations make these winter pansies such a popular choice for livening up dull days. Even severe frosts will not entirely put a stop to their flowering. 15cm/6in

◆ *Very attractive winter hanging baskets may be made using these pansies tightly packed together to create a ball of colour.*

*Limnanthes douglasii* Sunny little flowers, frequently referred to as poached egg plants, are ideal as an edging to a border from early summer. Allow them to self-seed from one year to the next. ○, 15cm/6in

*Calendula officinalis* All of the true marigolds, like this particular variety, are noted for the simplicity and ease with which they may be cultivated, flowering from spring to autumn. ○, 45 × 30cm/1¹/₂ × 1ft

*Gazania 'Dorothy'* A South African daisy available in a whole range of colours to include, of course, this buttery yellow one. Position in a sunny place for the flowers to open. ○, 30 × 20cm/1ft × 8in

*Chrysanthemum parthenium* Noted for distinctly aromatic leaves and flowers of a long-lasting quality. Ideal as an edging plant, perhaps to line a path. ○, 23 × 15cm/ 9 × 6in

*Viola* **'Sorbet Mixed'** So many very different strains of pansy from which to choose, none of which ever looks out of place when positioned casually among other more permanent plantings. 10 × 30cm/4in × 1ft

◆ *Why not edge a path, or border the wall of a house, with small clay pots, each one containing a pansy plant?*

***Godetia*** Chalice-shaped flowers, sometimes single, sometimes double, make not only splendid border plants but are useful for cutting or for growing as colourful pot plants with which to decorate the house. 20–30cm/8–12in

***Schizanthus × wintonensis* 'Hit Parade'** The poor man's orchid deserves to be among the most beautiful of all annuals, smothered as it is with airy flowers over feathery, ferny foliage. ○, 30cm/1ft

***Salvia splendens*** Perhaps it is the uniformity and compactness of the plant of this tender salvia which contribute towards its widespread use. Scarlet blooms never fail to make an impact. ○, 30cm/1ft

***Nemesia*** Shown here in shades of orange and red, nemesia will trail a blaze of colour through the border. It makes, too, a suitable subject for pots and containers. ○, 30–45cm/1–1$^{1}/_{2}$ft

**Salpiglossis 'Casino'** Trumpet-shaped flowers in vibrant colour mixes make these showy annuals strong candidates for any scheme where a bold effect is looked for. Suitable for cutting, they are somewhat sticky to handle. ○, 60–90cm/2–3ft

◆ *All of the annuals described on these pages are as suitable for containers as they are for cultivation in the open ground.*

A border like this one, closely packed with summer-flowering fuchsias, provides non-stop colour for the greater part of the summer. It should be remembered, of course, that an effect of this kind is dependent upon generous quantities of plant material.

◆ *Cuttings of fuchsias are easily taken during the spring and summer using non-flowering shoots. Rooting should take place within two weeks.*

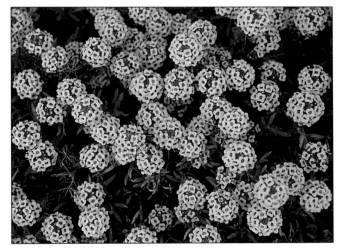

***Lobularia maritima (Alyssum maritimum)*** Often used as an edging plant, particularly in those parks and gardens where bedding-out schemes are the order of the day. Available also in pink and lilac. ○, 3in/7.5cm

***Osteospermum* 'Whirligig'** Beautifully shaped, sophisticated flowers for an open, sunny position. Although there are hardy osteospermums, most are unlikely to survive extremes of cold. ○, 30 × 30cm/1 × 1ft

***Senecio maritima*** Silver-leafed cineraria is a deservedly popular annual grown for its ornamental, deeply-cut foliage. Here it is placed as a spot plant among highly charged, bedding begonias. A foil of this kind provides rest to the eye. ◯, 30 × 30cm/1 × 1ft

◆ *Combinations of the kind shown here work equally as well in pots and containers and may be varied throughout the seasons.*

***Impatiens*** Vibrant busy lizzies are not for those who yearn for quiet, understated schemes. However, free-flowering as they are, they may be relied upon for colour all summer. 30 × 15cm/1ft × 6in

***Ageratum*** Powdery flowers of purplish-blue bring a different form and colour to bedding-out schemes. Coming into flower early on, ageratum will continue in bloom until autumn. ◯, 15cm/6in

# *Alpines and Rock Plants – Tiny Treasures*

Of course alpines and rock plants lend themselves to the small garden. These are tiny little bulbs, perennials, shrubs, and even trees, which on account of their size sit comfortably and are at home in a small-scale landscape. They belong at the front of the border, in specially prepared rock gardens, on scree beds and in troughs, old sinks, pots and any other suitable container.

In the main they share a dislike of winter wet and are happiest when planted in free draining soil. To achieve this, heavy clay, or similar, should be broken down with the addition of generous quantities of grit. A sleeve of gravel placed around the throat of the plant will also aid drainage.

There is something immensely satisfying about rock gardening. Maybe it is a desire to play Gulliver, to experience a miniature world where we can create mountains and valleys, forests and plains and nurture seemingly frail and vulnerable plants into life.

This well furnished rock garden succeeds on account of the fact that it has been created mindful of scale. Stone has been used boldly and in such a way as to suggest a stratum of natural outcrop. Plantings too are purposeful and in harmony.

◆ *Note here how the rock has been layered and set into the soil. Avoid placing stone at random.*

***Aubrieta* 'Barker's Double'** Aubrieta here is positioned in such a way as to spill over the rock face to provide a dramatic contrast with the grey stone. A good form of a familiar plant, flowering from spring into early summer. ○, 5 × 45cm/2in × 1¹/₂ft

◆ *Once the flowering period is over, cut back really hard. In a short while a tidy mound of fresh foliage will appear.*

***Iberis priutii*** Startlingly white flowers in late spring to early summer over dark, evergreen foliage, the whole appearing to come from some tiny crevice in the wall. ○, 15 × 45cm/ 6in × 1¹/₂ft

◆ *Too often good garden plants are shunned because they are considered to be ordinary. This is a mistake for they often act as a foil to the less common.*

***Sanguinaria canadensis* 'Plena'**
Snowy-white flowers of the blood-root appear in the early part of spring. They are slow to establish and go over quickly. ◑, 10cm/4in

***Ipheion uniflorum* 'Violaceum'** An enchanting perennial bulb with starry spring flowers of the palest of violets. Mark the spot for ipheion dies down completely by summer. 15cm/6in

***Iris pumila*** Note how this miniature iris has spread through the gravel where it obviously is enjoying a sun-baked position. Flowers mid-spring. 10cm/4in

***Lithodora diffusa* 'Star'** Irresistible. In early summer deep blue and white flowers marked, as its name implies, with a star formation. Lithodora prefers acidic conditions which may easily be created wtihin an alpine or rock garden. 15cm/6in

◆ *Soil is measured for alkalinity or acidity on a pH scale. Neutral is a pH of 7.0, above is alkaline, below acid.*

***Tulipa batalinii*** This miniature tulip originates in Central Asia. Above grey-green, wavy leaves rise soft, pale yellow flowers in spring. 10cm/4in

***Corydalis flexuosa*** It is hardly surprising that this striking blue flower has become increasingly popular in recent years. A number of named forms exist. Flowers late spring. 30 × 30cm/1 × 1ft

***Dicentra cucullaria*** A dainty white form of bleeding heart that is probably best grown in a pot containing a mixture of gritty soil. Spring-flowering. 15cm/6in

***Penstemon menziesii*** Oval-shaped green leaves clothe a series of shrubby stems above which are massed violet-blue flowers. The flowers of this penstemon, which is one of many suitable for the rock garden, open in early summer. Constant dead-heading will make for a succession of blooms. 15 × 30cm/6in × 1ft

◆ *Delay cutting back all penstemons until the spring. The previous year's growth will afford them some winter protection.*

197

Double primulas, like this one, have become very collectable and are prized additions to the rock garden, particularly where they can enjoy both semi-shade and humus-rich soil. Periodically, following flowering in spring, they should be divided. 10cm/4in

Eastertime is synonymous with the flowering of the pasque flower, *Pulsatilla vulgaris*. The long, drooping bell-shaped blooms last for weeks, particularly when dead-heading is carried out, and are followed by most appealing seedheads.

Flowering at the same time is the showy little celandine in one of its cultivated forms. *Ranunculus* 'Brazen Hussey' well lives up to its name with its bold and brassy yellow flowers and deep bronze foliage. Mark its position for it disappears completely as the year progresses.

Everyone is familiar with the primrose at home in woodlands and upon banksides. Less commonly known is *Primula* 'Hose-in-Hose' where the usual primrose flower is surrounded by a ruff of miniature leaves.

***Phlox bifida*** Another rockery phlox seen growing against and toning with a slate division. Although full of grey-blue flowers, it is noticeable how many buds are yet to open. ○, E, 10 × 30cm/4in × 1ft

**Mossy saxifrage** All of the mossy saxifrages are entirely satisfactory for spreading out to cover the ground with low hummocks of fresh green foliage. These pretty flowers appear in the spring. Take the trouble to dead head. E, 15 × 30cm/6in × 1ft

***Phlox subulata* 'Betty'** Low-growing phlox create a spreading carpet of flowers in the late spring and early summer. Here 'Betty' is a mass of deep pink blooms completely masking the foliage. ○, E, 10 × 30cm/4in × 1ft

***Daphne cneorum*** On a still evening the perfume of this lovely, prostrate daphne will fill the entire garden. Rich pink flowers are carried above tiny evergreen leaves in spring. Plant in a sunny spot which attracts some shade. E, 45 × 90cm/1¹/₂ × 3ft

◆ *Small shrubs, and even tiny trees, will give the rock garden a degree of structure and will help to maintain interest out of season.*

***Aethionema* 'Warley Rose'** This compact shrub, smothered in soft pink flowers during the early summer, is semi-evergreen. As it is short-lived, take replacement cuttings periodically. ○, 15 × 23cm/6 × 9in

***Androsace lanuginosa*** A pretty mat-forming perennial with a trailing habit which will be in bloom for much of the summer. 5 × 30cm/2in × 1ft

201

*Ajuga* **'Pink Surprise'** Bugle is often thought of as having a blue flower. An excellent carpet of foliage with flowers in spring. E, 15 × 60cm/ 6in × 2ft

◆ *Attention to detail will improve the appearance of the garden. Frequent dead-heading will help to maintain a neat effect.*

*Brunnera macrophylla* **(Siberian bugloss)** Strong green leaves form a splendid background and remain good when the spring flowers are spent. ◑, 45 × 45cm/1¹/₂ × 1¹/₂ft

*Lamium roseum* **'Wootton Pink'** (pictured left) An absolutely charming combination of clear pink flowers in late spring over gently variegated leaves. This variety of dead-nettle will delight as a non-invasive form of ground cover. 15 × 30cm/6in × 1ft

*Epimedium* × *youngianum* **'Roseum'** Enjoy these interesting little flowers in the first part of the year. The leaves develop to become quite bronze in autumn. 25 × 30cm/10in × 1ft

◆ *Over winter cut all epimediums hard back to ground level to ensure that new flowers are clear of all old growth.*

***Alchemilla conjuncta*** Prettily shaped, silky leaves, edged in white, combine with sprays of lime-green flowers from mid to late summer. Plant singly or to drift at the front of a border. 15 × 30cm/6in × 1ft

***Alchemilla erythropoda*** A miniature lady's mantle which possesses all the good qualities of its larger cousin, *A. mollis*, but never the sometimes tiresome habit of seeding around so freely as to become a nuisance. 15 × 30cm/ 6in × 1ft

***Euphorbia myrsinites*** Place this spurge in such a way as to allow it to drape over rocks or hang down the side of a low wall. Appearing in spring at the tips of fleshy, glaucous foliage are lime bracts. ○, E, 15 × 60cm/6in × 2ft

◆ *Most alpine plants enjoy a sunny situation. When siting a rock or alpine garden, bear this in mind.*

*Gentiana sino-ornata* Bright blue flowers for the autumn. However, this gentian is fairly demanding and must be provided with moist, acid soil and positioned in sun. 7.5 × 23cm/3 × 9in

*Campanula garganica* Some of the small campanulas can prove troublesome by running. Not so garganica which forms tight rosettes of leaves against which are displayed blue starry flowers in summer. Most effective with sandstone. 15 × 30cm/6in × 1ft

*Campanula* '**Birch Hybrid**' A cross between *C. portenschlagiana* and the familiar *C. poscharskyana*, 'Birch Hybrid' is a quick growing, versatile plant to flower mid to late summer and, maybe, again later. 15 × 30cm/6in × 1ft

*Omphalodes cappadocica* '**Cherry Ingram**' An excellent named form to produce a mass of eye-catching blue flowers all the way through the spring. 15 × 30cm/ 6in × 1ft

***Ramonda myconi*** Few alpines succeed in total shade. Ramonda is an exception and will be perfectly happy in the shadow of a peat-block wall where it will thrive in the acidic conditions. Flowers late spring/early summer. ●, E, 7.5 × 15cm/3 × 6in

***Erinus alpinus*** Grow this tiny rock plant in an old sink or a trough or allow it to seed around a gravel garden. Flowers in late spring and summer are combinations of red, mauve, pink or white. ○, E, 7.5 × 7.5cm/3 × 3in

***Erigeron karvinskianus*** Start this delightful self-seeder off in the rock garden and then watch the way it will place itself, always with style, in cracks, crevices or wherever it can gain a foothold. Flowers summer to autumn. ○, 15 × 30cm/6in × 1ft

***Armeria maritima*** Do not give this pin-cushion of thrift too great a richness. It will thrive in fairly poor soil to produce in summer a succession of little rounded, pink flowers. Look out for a white form. ○, E, 10 × 20cm/ 4 × 8in

*Dianthus* **'Gravetye Gem'** Plant pinks not just on account of their scented flowers in summer but also for their rather spiky leaves which form a pleasing contrast with much other foliage. Give them an open, free-draining site. ○, E, 20 × 30cm/8in × 1ft

◆ *It is important when placing plants to give consideration as much to texture and form as to flower. Care should be taken to avoid any kind of sameness.*

*Dianthus* **'Rose de Mai'** An abundance of summer flower such as is displayed here makes this old-fashioned pink a worthy choice for any garden. Pinks root very easily from cuttings. ○, E, 20 × 45cm/8in × 1¹/₂ft

*Convolvulus sabatius* Allow this non-invasive convolvulus to trail its lavender-blue flowers across the border in summer and early autumn. Not reliably hardy in cold areas where it should be overwintered in a pot under glass. ○, 15 × 45cm/6in × 1¹/₂ft

# Bulbs – All Year Fillers

Bulbs are rather like miniature spires, particularly at the start of the year when they appear to soar above otherwise dormant plantings to bring borders alive with splashes of colour and interest during somewhat grey and sombre months. But they are not just for the late winter and early spring. From the first snowdrops in late winter to nerines in autumn there are countless bulbs from which to choose to give glamour and excitement to even the smallest of gardens.

The secret is to pack them in. Plant in generous groups to fill gaps between existing perennials, to carpet the bare undersides of deciduous shrubs and trees, to complement and contrast with evergreens as well as to provide a changing focal pattern of pots on terrace or patio.

Generally bulbs enjoy good drainage. If your soil is heavy, or inclined to be water-logged, incorporate plenty of horticultural grit into the planting compost. In some instances it may be a good idea to rest the bulb itself on a layer of grit or gravel.

**Cyclamen coum** Even without their pretty late winter pink or white flowers, these cyclamen are highly desirable for their interestingly marbled leaves. Plant them to colonize a dry situation where little else would happily thrive. ◑, 10cm/4in

◆ *Despite their rather fragile appearance, cyclamen are, in fact, remarkably hardy and will easily defy the very worst of winter weather.*

***Crocus tommasinianus*** Make a small space for these early spring flowers where they may be left undisturbed to naturalize. Ideally they should be planted in such a way as to suggest a random drift. 10cm/4in

**Dutch crocus** The splendid, large heads of these versatile spring bulbs demand to be noticed. Crocus, as these, may be grown in the open ground, in either sun or shade, or massed in pots. 10cm/4in

***Anemone blanda* 'White Splendour'** Caught in a moment of spring sunshine, these woodland anemones positively glow among the lower branches of a chaenomeles. As the quince flowers open to steal centre-stage, so those of the anemone will fade. 10cm/4in

◆ *This kind of thoughtful planting demonstrates just one of the ways in which bulbs may be used to form part of an on-going succession of colour throughout the year.*

*Narcissus cyclamineus* A long, protruding trumpet is a distinctive feature of this early spring daffodil. 15–20cm/6–8in

*Narcissus bulbocodium* No garden should be without daffodils in springtime. Where space is at a premium miniature varieties, like this one, are ideal. ○, 15–20cm/6–8in

◆ *Plant bulbs from late summer onwards for display the following year.*

*Narcissus 'February Gold'* Of all the miniature daffodils this remains, deservedly, a firm favourite. An excellent choice for pot cultivation. 15–20cm/6–8in

**Narcissus 'Hawera'** A small gravel garden is enlivened in spring with the addition of bulbs. 'Hawera' thrives in this well-drained situation. 45cm/1¹/₂ft

**Hyacinthoides italica** Used as spring bedding here, these scented hyacinths would look equally good placed in a large container. 20cm/8in

**Erythronium 'Citronella'** Wonderful pale lemon spring flowers rise in clumps over interestingly veined leaves. The dog's tooth violet dies down in early summer. 15cm/6in

◆ *Erythroniums are available in a number of named forms. These include 'Pagoda', 'Pink Perfection', 'Rose Queen' and 'White Beauty'.*

***Tulipa* 'Keizerskroon'** This neglected corner has been brought to life with an effective association of tulips with primrose 'White Shades'. 45cm/1¹/₂ft

◆ *Obviously bedding like this is very much for spring. Another scheme will need to be substituted for later on.*

***Muscari neglectum*** Spring-flowering grape hyacinths with their dense spikes of blue will readily increase in most situations and are useful for filling awkward corners. Bulbs are best planted in the autumn. 10–15cm/4–6in

***Tulipa* 'Maréchal Niel'** An imaginative and sophisticated spring bedding scheme. The pale gold of the tulip has been artfully chosen to pick up and reflect the eye of the Universal pansy. 45cm/1¹/₂ft

◆ *Such a planting as this has a vitality and freshness which is very much in keeping with the time of year.*

***Anemone nemorosa* 'Robinsoniana'** It is difficult to resist this lovely, pale lavender form of the spring-flowering wood anemone. Absolutely charming in a natural setting which may be no more than around the bole of a tree. 15cm/6in

◆ *Anemones should be left undisturbed to establish themselves in colonies.*

**Tulipa 'Black Parrot'** These velvety parrot tulips form an integral part of a small yew enclosed garden. By planting them tightly together a limited number assumes an air of dramatic and visual importance. 45cm/1½ft

◆ *Traditionally tulips are lifted once the spring flowering season is over. By planting them deeply they may be left in situ to flower for many years to come.*

**Fritillaria imperialis** Crown imperials, in orange, red or yellow, are amongst the most striking of spring bulbs. Use them to give height to the border. Best results are achieved in very well drained soil. 1m × 30cm/3 × 1ft

**Fritillaria pyrenaica** Moody, deep purple bells tinged greenish-gold make an unusual addition to the spring garden. Bulbs, grown in sun, are best planted in position in the autumn. 30cm/1ft

***Iris sibirica*** All the sibirica irises succeed best in moisture retentive soil. Indeed, they associate well with water and are totally in keeping beside the pond or in the bog garden. Flowers in early summer. ◯, 60 × 60cm/2 × 2ft

***Allium aflatunense*** **'Purple Sensation'** Taking up very little space, these splendid ornamental onions should be placed to rise through and above other summer plantings. All of the alliums are excellent for drying. 1m/3ft

***Nectaroscordum siculum*** Gracefully arching umbels of distinctive soft green and white flowers are the hallmark of these uncommon but easy bulbs. Grow in full sun or part shade through other foliage plants. 1m/3ft

***Gladiolus byzantinus*** A small-flowered, early gladiolus which is sufficiently hardy to remain in the ground. For a sensational combination, plant in drifts among the lower branches of *Cornus controversa* 'Variegata'. 60cm/2ft

**Eremurus bungei** Foxtail lilies make a bold statement in mid-summer. They are probably most successful when grouped at the back of the border. ○, 1.5m × 60cm/5 × 2ft

**Lilium martagon var. album** Turk's cap lilies are easily grown in a semi-shaded position. The white form introduces welcome coolness during hot days of summer. 1.5m × 30cm/ 5 × 1ft

◆ *The more widely grown* L. martagon *will bear in excess of twenty purple flowers on a single stem in mid-summer.*

**Allium moly** An additional bonus to this brightly coloured, summer-flowering yellow onion is that it is scented. Its small size makes it especially useful for the rock garden. 25cm/10in

◆ *Dead head all bulbs as the flowers finish and then allow the leaves to die down naturally. The advantage of planting bulbs amongst other perennials and shrubs is that their decaying foliage is soon masked.*

***Lilium regale*** The intoxicating fragrance of the regal lily is one of the delights of summer. Do not worry if you cannot find space in the border for they do particularly well when cultivated in pots. 1.2m × 30cm/4 × 1ft

◆ *Lilies require well drained soil, water during the growing season and a position in full sun. Surround bulbs with a little sharp sand at planting time.*

***Lilium 'King Pete'*** Creamy orange flowers are nicely speckled with purple on this sturdy, upright lily. 'King Pete' is but one of many Asiatic hybrids from which to choose for summer flowers. 'Connecticut King', 'Sterling Silver' and 'Cote d'Azur' are among the most popular.
1m × 30cm/3 × 1ft

*Agapanthus* **Headbourne Hybrids** This strain of blue African lily looks remarkably exotic but is actually quite hardy. Grow agapanthus either in the open ground or in pots where they may be sited for greatest impact when in flower in late summer. ○, 60 × 45cm/2 × 1¹/₂ft

*Eucomis bicolor* Although the pineapple plant is unlikely to come through the severest of winters, it is well worth finding a sunny spot for it to appreciate the charm of its unusual green flowers in summer. ○, 45 × 60cm/1¹/₂ × 2ft

**Autumn crocus** Surprisingly, even when planted in autumn, these end-of-year crocus will flower within three to four weeks. Use them to add a touch of brilliance to the final days of the dying year. 10cm/4in

*Nerine bowdenii* Gorgeously ostentatious bulbs from South Africa which come into their own as the season draws to a close. Planted in full sun, where the bulbs may be baked, they are reliably hardy. ○, 45 × 20cm/1¹/₂ft × 8in

***Crinum powellii*** Plant in humus-rich, well drained soil at the base of a sunny wall or fence for these beautiful, scented flowers to give of their best in autumn.
○, 1m × 60cm/3 × 2ft

***Dahlia 'Gerrie Hoek'*** All of the late-flowering dahlias bring much needed warmth to the end of summer and autumn borders. Here the deep pink of 'Gerrie Hoek' tones with the crinums. ○, 60 × 60cm/2 × 2ft

***Colchicum speciosum*** Somewhat unusually colchicums may actually be grown 'dry' by placing the bulb without soil or water on a saucer. In the garden they require free draining soil in full sun. Autumn-flowering. ○, 20 × 20cm/8 × 8in

***Cyclamen hederifolium*** The pretty ivy-shaped leaves of these tiny cyclamen bridge the gap between autumn and winter. Flowers, which appear before the foliage, bloom during the autumn and are impervious to cold.
10 × 20cm/4 × 8in

# Water Plants – A Profusion of Flowers and Foliage

Virtually any water feature, irrespective of how tiny it may be, will, almost certainly, appear somewhat naked without a clothing of associated leaf and flower. In addition to those plants which actually grow in water, marginal plantings will contribute to the overall appearance of the water garden in two distinct ways. First, they will help to suggest a natural look, giving to the immediate area the semblance of fertile, moisture-retentive ground, maybe even going so far as to hint at a miniature bog garden. Second, they will have a totally functional purpose, that of disguising the very mechanics by which any artificial water system is created. Nothing, after all, is more unsatisfactory than a 'natural' pond whose liner is clearly visible.

Notwithstanding that in most small gardens the soil is most likely to be quite ordinary, neither particularly wet nor excessively dry, it is still possible to include a wide range of perennials which, grown around a pool or a stream, will not only look convincing but will perform well over an extended period of time.

***Primula sieboldii*** The outer sides of frilly edged petals are flushed pink and palest mauve on this slightly tender primula. Plant in damp soil in a position which is afforded some shelter. Flowers early summer. 20 × 30cm/8in × 1ft

***Primula florindae*** Tiny hanging bells of citrus-yellow carry with them a sweet scent. A small colony of this primula will bring colour to the garden for many weeks in summer. ◑, 75 × 75cm/2½ × 2½ft

*Primula pulverulenta* Grown in a mass, as pictured, this candelabra primula makes an exciting, eye-catching display during early summer. As is always the case, a group is much more effective than a solitary plant. 1m × 45cm/3 × 1½ft

*Primula japonica* **'Postford White'** A dark eye sets off the white petals of the open flower which, in bud, is distinctly tinged with pink. Flowering in early summer in a semi-shaded position. 45 × 45cm/1½ × 1½ft

*Primula vialii* It is difficult not to be drawn to the remarkable poker flower heads of this very distinctive primula. Buds of bright scarlet slowly open to lavender in late spring. Position in rich, moist soil. 30 × 30cm/1 × 1ft

***Astilbe* × *arendsii* 'Erica'** All of the astilbes are noted for their feathery summer plumes and deeply cut foliage which very often will turn cigar-coloured as autumn approaches. They are unfussy as to soil conditions. 1 × 1m/3 × 3ft

***Geum* 'Red Wings'** A striking form of the popular and widely grown avens. Associating well with water, the geums are, in fact, content with any reasonably rich garden soil. Flowers appear in summer. ○, 30 × 30cm/1 × 1ft

***Astilbe* × *arendsii* 'Granat'** Deep, almost rust-red, flowers are a welcome change from pastel hues. Try this astilbe for a summer display in partnership with the Japanese blood grass, *Imperata cylindrica* 'Rubra', of a similar tone. 1 × 1m/ 3 × 3ft

***Geum rivale* 'Album'** A lovely, simple white form of avens which in this garden is planted against a background of many hanging, tubular *Polygonatum falcatum*. 60 × 60cm/ 2 × 2ft

**Lobelia 'Dark Crusader'** Such a handsome, richly-coloured perennial as this deserves to be given prominence in the garden. In cold areas cover the crowns over winter with a mulch of compost or old fern leaves. Flowers late summer. 1m × 30cm/3 × 1ft

◆ *Make a space too for* L. cardinalis *'Queen Victoria' whose foliage, above which rise scarlet flowers, is of a deep burgundy red.*

**Mimulus** Often characterized by their spotted markings mimulus, like this hybrid, flower in summer but require soil conditions which remain damp throughout the year. Cut to the ground in autumn. 30 × 30cm/1 × 1ft

**Camassia leichtlinii** Violet-blue flowers rise in early summer above the foliage in this moisture-loving perennial. Its native habitat is among wet grasslands which remain moist at all times. 75 × 30cm/2½ × 1ft

**Arisaema candidissimum** Any amount of care and attention is worth it to cultivate these wonderfully exotic plants which flower, before the leaves fully mature, in the early summer. 30 × 30cm/1 × 1ft

**Dodecatheon meadia** Another extraordinary flower in terms of colour, markings and shape. The shooting star, the name by which it is commonly known, is a beautiful plant for a damp spot. Spring-flowering. 45 × 30cm/1½ × 1ft

*Schizostylis coccinea* Kaffir lilies, blooming from late summer well into autumn, add a touch of brightness at a time when colours are becoming more subdued. Enjoying moist conditions, they will also flourish in normal garden soil. 60 × 30cm/2 × 1ft

*Filipendula rubra* **'Venusta'** Tall-growing meadow-sweet carrying plentiful heads of the softest pink in mid-summer. Meadow-sweet can seed around to become something of a nuisance so remove spent flowers before they set seed. 2 × 1.2m/6 × 4ft

*Chaerophyllum hirsutum* **'Roseum'** Rather akin to cow parsley but with very delicate, palest pink umbels set above rosettes of leaves. The flowering period is during the late spring. 60 × 60cm/2 × 2ft

*Cardamine pratensis* **(Lady's smock)** A delightful clump-forming perennial whose lilac flowers open in early spring. 25 × 10cm/10 × 4in

***Caltha palustris*** It would be difficult not to include, if at all possible, the marsh marigold in the water garden. Use it as an edging to ponds or simply as a spring statement. ○, 30 × 45cm/1 × 1¹/₂ft

***Lysichiton americanus*** Wonderful yellow spathes belonging to the skunk cabbage are followed by huge paddle leaves. At the margins of the pond this will make a spectacular show in spring. But, be warned, it does need space. 1m × 75cm/3 × 2¹/₂ft

***Trollius europaeus*** Bright yellow heads of the globe flower produced in spring look best, where there is sufficient space, together as a group. Stocks may easily be increased by division in the autumn. 60 × 60cm/2 × 2ft

***Iris* 'Holden Clough'** Beautiful markings in early summer on the falls of this iris which thrives in damp soil make it a must. It is especially effective when planted with the golden-coloured grass, *Carex elata* 'Aurea', as pictured here. 75 × 75cm/2¹/₂ × 2¹/₂ft

*Iris sibirica* **'Soft Blue'** Clump-forming sibirica irises are most appealing border plants for early summer and are very much at home in association with water. Most nurseries will be able to offer a wide choice of colour. 1m × 60cm/3 × 2ft

*Trillium grandiflorum* **'Roseum'** Rich soil, shade from the sun and immense patience are required if the desperately slow-to-establish wake-robin is to reward in spring with such lovely flowers as these. ●, 38 × 30cm/15 × 12in

*Iris missouriensis* Obviously a small garden will not permit, in terms of room alone, growing such a stand of irises as is shown here in early summer. What is important, though, is to aim for bold effects rather than unco-ordinated mixes. 60 × 60cm/2 × 2ft

◆ *The beauty of irises is that their foliage continues to hold interest long after the flowers, which should be cut off as they die, are over.*

***Houttuynia cordata* 'Chameleon'** It has to be admitted that this multi-coloured, ground covering perennial will, given the right conditions, spread more than is always desirable. That said, it is not at all difficult to control. ○, 10cm/4in

◆ *If these rather off-beat colours appeal, but space is really restricted, then grow houttuynia in a pot where it will put on a good show for several months.*

***Matteuccia struthiopteris*** For sheer elegance and style make room for some decorative ferns. This ostrich fern is particularly attractive when the new fronds unfurl in springtime. 1m × 60cm/3 × 2ft

***Rodgersia sambucifolia*** Large-leafed rodgersias do, naturally, take up space. However, they are useful statement plants and serve a purpose in helping to define a planting scheme. This one has finely marked leaves. 1 × 1m/3 × 3ft

***Hosta sieboldiana*** The glaucous leaves of this hosta create interest from the point at which they open in the spring until the moment when, caught by frost, they collapse at the year's end. ◑, 75 × 75cm/2¹/₂ × 2¹/₂ft

***Onoclea sensibilis*** Use this prettily shaped fern as a dainty edging to a small pool or tiny, trickling water course. New fronds emerge in the spring when old growth may be cut back. 45 × 60cm/1¹/₂ × 2ft

Use hostas, such as this splendid *H.* 'Halcyon' illustrated here, throughout the water garden to add form to other less definite plantings and, of course, to act as ground cover. Flowers, which may at times appear a little insignificant, are an additional bonus in mid-summer. Some hostas, like 'Krossa Regal', may be grown quite happily in containers.

***Aponogeton distachyos*** Include plants like the water hawthorn in a small pond to assist with the oxygenation of the water. White flowers throughout the summer possess distinctive black centres. Plant in up to 45cm/1¹/₂ft of water.

***Myriophyllum aquaticum*** Parrot's feather, the more convenient name by which it is known, thrives beneath the surface where it helps to keep the water clear.

***Orontium aquaticum*** Another oxygenating plant but one with rather unusual, poker-like flowers of creamy-white tipped yellow which extend over and above the leaves in spring. Place this plant in up to 30cm/1ft of water.

◆ *In order to buy plants like this one it may be necessary to go to a garden centre which specializes in the sale of plants for water.*

***Nymphaea* 'James Brydon'** Somewhat surprisingly these flowers, which appear over deep green leaves, are fragrant. Divide lilies every few years in the spring. Planting depth 23–45cm/9in–1¹/₂ft

***Nymphaea* 'Laydekeri Fulgens'** These richly coloured flowers have spread to fill this small pool. Usually lilies will flower from early summer until the first frosts of autumn. Planting depth 23cm/9in or more.

***Nymphaea* 'Marliacea Albida'** A pure white, scented lily with very pronounced yellow stamens. As with all water lilies, plant in still water in full sun. Planting depth 45cm/1¹/₂ft

***Nymphaea* 'Marliacea Chromatella'** Flowers of deep, buttery yellow are set off by leaves which, spotted brown and bronze, are olive-green in colour. Planting depth 45cm/1¹/₂ft

Fill attractive pots and containers on a seasonal basis.
Here the early-flowering *Iris reticulata* will bring cheer to
the cold days of late winter. After flowering the bulbs
may be stored and the pot replanted.

# Through the Seasons

The owner of any small garden must endeavour to sustain interest the whole year round. Unlike a larger garden, where certain areas are designed for a particular season and are then succeeded by somewhere else, and where the whole can seldom be seen together, the small garden is, most often, on view at all times. For that reason it cannot be that any part, however apparently insignificant, can be set aside, overlooked or ignored.

Instead the gardener must work hard to achieve continuity, to provide for a successional series of highlights, so that as one planting goes over another comes into its own. This is not, it must be admitted, always easy to achieve. But it can be done. It requires a sound knowledge of plants, skill in their arrangement, effective husbandry, a critical eye and close attention to detail. It demands patience, a flexible approach, imagination, good judgement and common sense. That said, the results will amply repay the time and effort spent.

Key trees, shrubs and perennials will all play a part. They will be those which, for whatever reason, contribute to the overall garden scene in more than a single way. It may be that they fruit as well as flower, or that interesting foliage turns colour later on, or that bark takes on a prominence in winter. It could be no more than the effect of frost on an evergreen or the continuous flowering of a perennial. What matters, in a small space, is to consider carefully the merits of all plants chosen for the garden so that whatever the season there is something over which to pause, to reflect upon or, indeed, to marvel at.

*Erica carnea* **'Myretoun Ruby'** Winter-flowering heathers will bloom continuously during the months of winter and early spring. After flowering cut back hard to encourage new, fresh green growth which will remain good all year. E, 30 × 45cm/1 × 1¹/₂ft

*Bergenia purpurascens* These handsome leaves are in their winter livery. As the days warm they will revert to green and produce richly-coloured flowers in spring. A perennial to contrast with other foliage plants. E, 30 × 45cm/ 1 × 1¹/₂ft

*Hedera helix* **'Cristata'** Include this restrained ivy for its very prettily shaped leaves. An ideal choice where a plain green background is required to set off more colourful plantings. E, 2.7m/9ft

*Hedera helix* **'Buttercup'** Warm yellows and golds, found in this evergreen ivy, will lighten with sunshine even the dullest of corners. Such intensity of colour is especially effective out of season. E, 2.7m/9ft

*Hedera helix* **'Glacier'** Ivies do not, of course, have to be grown as climbers. This one, with pronounced cream markings, would make an effective ground cover in a position of semi-shade. E, 2.7m/9ft

*Hedera helix* **'Goldheart'** Grown well, in a sunny position, 'Goldheart' will provide a splash of welcome colour all through the year. Cut out any stems which revert to green. E, 2.7m/9ft

***Ilex aquifolium* 'Ferox Argentea'** All the evergreen hollies, and this one is no exception, make for interesting backdrops against which other plants may be placed. Here an imaginative scheme could be developed by picking up on the cream variegation. E, 2.4 × 2.4m/8 × 8ft

◆ *Most hollies will respond to clipping and may, therefore, be transformed into balls or pyramids as well as unusual and creative topiary shapes.*

***Acer shirasawanum aureum*** A golden-leafed Japanese maple to act as a beacon of brilliance from spring until autumn. Position in a semi-shaded spot to avoid leaf scorch at the height of summer. ◑, 3 × 2.4m/10 × 8ft

***Aucuba japonica* 'Gold Dust'** Of value inasmuch as this shrub will succeed even in quite deep shade where it will produce a succession of red berries from autumn through to the spring. E, 2.4 × 2.4m/8 × 8ft

*Artemisia* **'Powis Castle'** A lovely silver-leafed shrub which is a perfect foil for pale pinks, blues and rich purples. Evergreen foliage should be hard pruned in spring when it will rapidly rejuvenate. ○, E, 1 × 1.2m/3 × 4ft

*Euonymus fortunei* **'Silver Queen'** Another shrub tolerant of some shade. Light variegation of creamy-white, especially startling in winter, would form a splendid background for a dark-flowered climber. E, 1 × 1.5m/ 3 × 5ft

*Hebe pinguifolia* **'Pagei'** Grey-green leaves, which remain attractive all year, are smothered in spring with tiny white flowers. Use as ground cover to carpet a difficult or neglected corner. E, 30cm × 1m/1 × 3ft

***Helictotrichon sempervirens*** Enjoy these graceful plumes by placing this non-spreading grass in a sunny position. Slender blue grey leaves are attractive at all times. Cut to the ground each spring. ○, 1.2m × 30cm/4 × 1ft

***Festuca ovina*** A very pretty, clump-forming silvery grass to use as a spot plant or as a tidy edging to path or border. Grasses all contribute year-round interest. ○, 25 × 30cm/ 10in × 1ft

***Stachys byzantina*** For most of the year grey, woolly lamb's ears form an effective carpet to spread around the base of contrasting shrubs such as *Berberis* 'Rose Glow'. ○, E, 45 × 30cm/1½ × 1ft

***Ballota pseudodictamnus*** Prune this pretty little shrublet each spring to retain its health and vigour. From the Mediterranean region, it is best positioned in sun on well drained soil. ○, E, 30 × 45cm/1 × 1½ft

***Abelia schumanii*** Warm flowers of mauve–pink are produced over a long period from summer into autumn. This is a shrub to associate with grey and silver leafed plants in a soft, muted scheme. Semi-E, 1.5 × 1.5m/5 × 5ft

***Indigofera heterantha*** A long flowering season, from midsummer through until autumn, makes this compact shrub worthy of a place in the small garden. It prefers to be placed in a sunny spot. ○, 2 × 2m/6 × 6ft

***Euphorbia dulcis* 'Chameleon'** Deep, mysterious purple foliage gradually changes through green to orange-red as the year progresses. A most striking plant which will oblige with seedlings to be found round and about. 40 × 40cm/ 16 × 16in

***Allium schoenoprasum* 'Forescate'** Pink flowered chives are not only good to cook with, but also make an attractive edging plant. Cut to the ground as flowers die and within a short time new foliage, and more flowers, will appear. 30 × 30cm/1 × 1ft

**Clematis 'Dr. Ruppel'** With so many lovely clematis to choose from, select those, like this one, which will flower freely throughout the summer. Strong colours need to be placed carefully. Height depends on soil and situation.

**Rosa 'Cornelia'** Within a small space, where every plant must earn its keep, it is important to make effective choices. This hybrid musk rose will flower all summer and is ideal for including in a mixed border. ○, 1.2 × 1.2m/ 4 × 4ft

**Lavatera 'Barnsley'** A shrubby mallow for a sunny, open spot in free-draining soil. Given these conditions 'Barnsley' will reward with a profusion of pale pink flowers for several months in summer. ○, 2 x 1m/6 x 3ft

***Escallonia* 'Iveyi'** A handsome shrub which is easily kept within bounds by judicious pruning. White flowers in mid to late summer are easily teamed with a contrasting clematis. E, 4 × 3m/13 × 10ft

***Hydrangea quercifolia*** Distinctive oak-like leaves give this splendid shrub its name. These white flower panicles which appear mid-summer will in time turn pink as the leaves colour to a vivid red-orange in the autumn. 2 × 2.4m/ 6 × 8ft

***Leucothöe fontanesiana*** Graceful, arching stems carry lustrous leaves which in shade remain green but which in a more open situation colour reddish-purple. Racemes of tiny white flowers appear in mid/late spring. For lime-free soil. E, 1.5 × 3m/5 × 10ft

***Epimedium* × *youngianum* 'Niveum'** Plant this delightful perennial in a partially shaded spot. After the delicate white spring flowers, prettily shaped leaves develop which colour well in the autumn. 25 × 30cm/10in × 1ft

***Pittosporum tenuifolium*** Highly ornamental, evergreen shrub which is much favoured by flower arrangers. Blackish stems carry pale green, variegated leaves. Plant away from cold winds in a sheltered, sunny site. E, 5 × 4m/16 × 13ft

◆ *None of the pittosporums is totally hardy but most should succeed in the warmth of an enclosed garden.*

***Clematis armandii*** Particularly welcome in the early spring for its wonderfully scented flowers. Once established, ever-green foliage will conceal an unsightly shed or clothe a trellis or pergola. ○, E, height depends on soil and situation.

***Eryngium tripartitum*** Steely-blue flowers rise above rather strange, thistle-type foliage throughout the mid-summer. Delay cutting back until spring so as to enjoy wonderful frosted effects. ○, 45 × 25cm/1¹/₂ft × 10in

***Helleborus foetidus* 'Wester Flisk'** All types of hellebore, without exception, are worth finding space for. This variety has grey-green leaves supported by red-tinged flower stalks in late winter/early spring. Plant in humus-rich soil in partial shade. ◑, E, 45 × 45cm/1¹/₂ × 1¹/₂ft

◆ *When tidying up hellebores in the early spring, look out for tiny self-sown seedlings. As they increase in size, pot on.*

***Rosa* 'Graham Thomas'** A new English rose which may be relied upon to bloom all through the summer and well into autumn. Prune in winter to encourage bushy growth and prevent wind rock. ○, 1.5 × 1m/5 × 3ft

***Erysimum* 'Bowles' Mauve'** Incredibly, this perennial wallflower is in bloom for virtually every month of the year. Renew plants periodically from cuttings to avoid the unsightly bare stems of older specimens. 60 × 60cm/ 2 × 2ft

***Pulsatilla vulgaris*** Pasque flowers, also in white and wine red, are charming in flower in the spring but appear equally attractive when the seedheads are allowed to develop. For a well drained site. 30 × 30cm/1 × 1ft

***Salvia officinalis* 'Purpurascens'** Leaves of purple, green and grey act as a foil to other plantings throughout the entire year. Spring pruning will help to retain compact growth and shape. O, E, 60cm x 1m/2 × 3ft

***Clematis* 'Lord Nevill'** Intense blue flowers appear not only during the early summer but for a second time in the autumn. Maximize shrubs as host plants for climbers, not least clematis. Height depends on soil and situation.

***Viola labradorica*** Allow this moody little viola to seed at will. Dark leafed foliage is near evergreen and sets off most effectively the tiny flowers of lilac, mauve and purple in spring and summer. 10 × 30cm/4in × 1ft

***Viburnum davidii*** A low-growing, spreading shrub of bold, dark green veined leaves which will thrive in awkward places. Autumn sees the development of turquoise-blue berries as an additional bonus. E, 90cm × 1.5m/3 × 5ft

***Viburnum tinus* 'Eve Price'** One of the most versatile of all shrubs. Easy to grow, the pink flowers appear, even in the coldest of weather, from autumn until spring. Evergreen foliage is constantly attractive. E, 2.4 × 2.4m/ 8 × 8ft

***Cotoneaster horizontalis*** In maturity this shrub develops an exciting framework as branches extend outward in the manner of a fishbone to form a giant fan. Rich autumn leaf colour combines with scarlet berries. 1.5 × 1.5m/ 5 × 5ft

◆ *Both bees and wasps are attracted to the somewhat insignificant flowers in summer bringing the whole shrub alive with murmurings.*

The simplicity of this variegated holly surrounded by box balls
is wholly matched in style and sophistication. An arrangement
of this kind forms a permanent and eye-catching feature.

# Index

*Aquilegia* hybrids

*Dicentra* 'Langtrees'

Spiral bay tree (*Laurus nobilis*) in lavender bed.

Peonies with yellow *Achillea* and mauve *Nepeta*